FATEH S CHAHAL

The Art of Attitude

Mastering Your Mindset for Success

Contents

Introduction

Welcome to "The Art of Attitude: Mastering Your Mindset for Success"! This book is for anyone who wants to achieve their goals and dreams in life by developing a winning mindset and attitude. This book aims to provide readers with the tools and strategies they need to cultivate a growth mindset, overcome limiting beliefs, and build resilience in the face of challenges.

Mindset and attitude are key factors that can impact success in every area of life, from personal relationships to professional achievements. A positive attitude and a growth mindset can lead to greater resilience, determination, and motivation, all of which are essential qualities for achieving success. Positive mindsets can give you the energy that you require to achieve your goals on time. A positive mindset can help individuals lead happier, healthier, and more fulfilling lives. Individuals can reap the many benefits of a positive mindset by cultivating gratitude, practising optimism, and focusing on solutions rather than problems.

In this book, we'll explore the two types of mindsets: fixed and growth. A fixed mindset is one in which individuals believe that their abilities and intelligence are fixed, and cannot be improved upon. They may believe that their success is determined by their innate abilities or talents, rather than their effort or hard work. Individuals with a fixed mindset may avoid challenges and risks, fearing failure and the potential for exposing their perceived limitations. In contrast, a growth mindset is one in which individuals believe that their abilities and intelligence can be developed through hard work, dedication, and perseverance. They view challenges as opportunities for growth and learning and are willing to take risks and try new things. By cultivating a growth mindset, readers can learn to embrace challenges, learn from failures, and continue to grow and develop throughout their lives.

We'll also cover practical strategies for developing a positive attitude, overcoming limiting beliefs, and building resilience. These strategies include cultivating gratitude, reframing negative thoughts, and developing coping mechanisms to overcome setbacks and challenges.

Throughout this book, readers will find real-life examples of people who have used their mindset and attitude to succeed personally and professionally. From athletes to entrepreneurs, these individuals have demonstrated the power of a growth mindset and a positive attitude to overcome obstacles and achieve their goals.

You will find repetitions of various explanations as to master your mindset for success you need to keep repeating your effectiveness. So whether you're looking to build your resilience, develop a growth mindset, or simply cultivate a more positive attitude, "The Art of Attitude: Mastering Your Mindset for Success" has something for you. Let's dive in and start mastering our mindsets for success!

* * *

1

Understanding Mindset

Explanation of Mindset

Mindset refers to the mental attitudes and beliefs that one holds about their abilities, intelligence, and potential for growth and development. These attitudes and beliefs are key in shaping a person's behaviour and actions, influencing how they approach challenges, opportunities, and setbacks in life.

In its true nature, Mindset is the lens through which individuals view themselves, others, and the world around them. It is shaped by a variety of factors including, personal experiences, cultural background, and social environment. It is an influencer for someone's thinking patterns, their emotions and it plays a significant role in determining their behaviour. Moreover, it starts to build in early childhood and can be impacted by several things such as praise and labels.

Another definition of Mindset can be one's orientation regarding the success that is embedded in their mind. If a person has a positive approach towards their goals and ambitions then it gets easier to attain them and the journey to achievement seems enjoyable, while on the other hand, a negative attitude towards one's goals mostly fails.

It all comes down to how you view yourself. Thinking profoundly about yourself will help you lead a better life than thinking poorly of yourself. A profound view of ourselves also enables us to develop a greater sense of self-awareness, which can help us to identify our strengths and weaknesses, set realistic goals, and make positive changes in our lives. It can help to develop a sense of purpose and meaning in our lives, which can provide the motivation and resilience needed to overcome challenges and achieve our goals.

Impact of Conscious and Subconscious Thoughts on Mindset

Our mindset is shaped not only by our conscious thoughts but also by our subconscious beliefs and attitudes. Both conscious and sub-conscious thoughts play a critical role in determining our mindset, influencing how we approach challenges, how we view our abilities and potential, and ultimately, how we experience and navigate the world around us.

Conscious thoughts are those that we are aware of and actively thinking about. These thoughts can be influenced by a variety of factors, including our past experiences, cultural background, and personal beliefs. When we consciously think about our abilities and potential, our thoughts can either be positive or negative. Positive thoughts can help us to develop a growth mindset, while negative thoughts can contribute to a fixed mindset.

Subconscious thoughts, on the other hand, are those that occur beneath our conscious awareness. These thoughts are shaped by our past experiences, beliefs, and attitudes and they can be difficult to change. Subconscious thoughts can influence our mindset in powerful ways, as they can shape our beliefs about ourselves and the world around us, without our conscious awareness.

For example, if someone has a subconscious belief that they are not good enough, this belief can undermine their efforts to develop a growth mindset, even if they consciously try to think positively about their abilities. Similarly, if someone has a subconscious belief that they are capable of achieving their goals, this belief can help to reinforce a growth mindset, even if they face setbacks along the way.

By becoming aware of our subconscious beliefs and working to shift them towards a more positive and growth-oriented mindset, we can develop the resilience and adaptability needed to thrive in today's rapidly changing world.

Overview of the two types of mindsets: Fixed and Growth

A fixed mindset is one in which individuals believe that their abilities and intelligence are fixed traits that cannot be changed or improved upon. They may believe that their success is determined by their innate abilities or talents, rather than their effort or hard work. Individuals with a fixed mindset may avoid challenges and risks, fearing failure and the potential for exposing their perceived limitations.

Individuals with a fixed mindset may be more resistant to change and less willing to take risks or try new approaches. They may be more likely to avoid challenges and responsibilities that they perceive as beyond their capabilities, which can limit their career advancement and professional development.

In contrast, a growth mindset is one in which individuals believe that their abilities and intelligence can be developed through hard work, dedication, and perseverance. They view challenges as opportunities for growth and learning and are willing to take risks and try new things. Individuals with a growth mindset understand that failure is a natural part of the learning process and that setbacks can be overcome with effort and persistence.

The impact of mindset on behaviour and actions can be seen in a variety of contexts. For example, in education, students with a growth mindset tend to be more engaged, motivated, and persistent in their learning compared to those with a fixed mindset. They are more likely to embrace challenges and view mistakes as opportunities for growth, which can lead to greater academic achievement over time.

Similarly, in sports and other competitive arenas, individuals with a growth mindset tend to perform better and be more resilient in the face of setbacks and failures. They are more likely to persist through difficult training regimens, take risks on the field, and recover quickly from losses or injuries.

In the workplace, mindset can also have a significant impact on job performance and career success. Individuals with a growth mindset tend to be more innovative, adaptable, and open to learning new skills and taking on new challenges. They are more likely to seek out feedback and use it constructively to improve their performances.

Let's discuss a Scenario: David and Sarah are both starting a running routine. David has a fixed mindset, while Sarah has a growth mindset.

David thinks to himself, "I'm not a runner, and I'm not very athletic. I'm not sure I'll be able to stick to this routine or make any real progress. I'll just give it a try and see what happens." David runs two miles at a slow pace and finds it challenging. He struggles to find the motivation to keep going and skips several runs throughout the week. When he doesn't see any significant improvement after a few weeks, he becomes discouraged and quits running altogether.

On the other hand, Sarah thinks, "I'm new to running, but I'm excited to give it a try and see how much progress I can make. I know it might be challenging, but I'm willing to put in the effort to improve." Sarah starts by running two miles at a slow pace and feels proud of herself for completing the run. She sets a goal for herself to run at least three times a week and gradually increases her distance and pace over time. When she has a bad day or a run that doesn't go as planned, she doesn't get discouraged. Instead, she sees it as an opportunity to learn and improve. She seeks advice from more experienced runners, tries new techniques and training methods, and pushes herself to keep going. Sarah eventually runs a 5k, then a 10k, and finally, a half marathon, setting new personal records along the way. Running becomes an integral part of Sarah's identity, and she continues to challenge herself and set new goals for herself.

In this scenario, David demonstrates a fixed mindset by seeing running as something he is either good at or not, with limited potential for improvement. This mindset leads to a lack of motivation, difficulty in sticking to the routine, and ultimately quitting when progress is slow or nonexistent. This mindset sabotages his health and happiness in the coming years of his age.

On the other hand, Sarah demonstrates a growth mindset by seeing running as a skill that can be developed through effort and dedication. She focuses on the process of improving her abilities and perseveres through setbacks and challenges. This mindset leads to motivation, resilience, and continued improvement over time. This mindset helped Sarah to be healthy and happy in her life.

How Does Mindset Affect Behavior and Actions?

Mindset can significantly impact behaviour and actions. A person's mindset can shape their attitudes, beliefs, and perceptions, which in turn can influence the decisions they make and the actions they take.

For example, if your behaviour is just towards proving how great you are rather than focusing on learning and getting better at something then you have a fixed mindset. While it is certainly gratifying to be recognized for our accomplishments and abilities, there is a danger in becoming overly focused on proving how great we are. This mindset can lead to a fixed mindset, in which we view our abilities as static and unchangeable, and we may be less willing to take risks or try new things, fearing failure or being perceived as less than perfect. In contrast, focusing on getting better rather than proving ourselves can foster a growth mindset.

Mindset can also affect how we view the success of others. Individuals with a fixed mindset may view the success of others as threatening or intimidating, believing that their own abilities are limited in comparison.

This can lead to a sad and unsatisfying life. Contrary to this, individuals with a growth mindset are more likely to view others succeeding as inspiring and motivating, with the faith that they too can triumph through hard work and dedication. They do not think that everyone can be as smart as Steve Jobs but they think that everyone can get smarter by working on themselves.

Mindset can have a significant impact on a person's behaviour and actions in a variety of contexts, including education, sports, and the workplace. Here are some ways in which mindset can affect one's conduct and functioning:

Motivation: Individuals with a growth mindset tend to be more motivated and persistent in pursuing their goals since they view challenges as opportunities for growth and learning and believe in development through hard work and dedication. They may be more likely to take on new challenges and push through difficult times, rather than giving up or becoming discouraged. They tend to be more focused on the process of achieving their goals, rather than the result. They are motivated by the progress and improvements they make along the way, rather than just the achievement of their goals. They are more likely to be self-motivated and persistent in pursuing their goals. They are motivated by a desire for self-improvement and personal growth and are willing to put in the effort and dedication necessary to achieve their goals. This can lead to greater success and fulfilment in all areas of their lives, as they can approach challenges with a positive and growth-oriented mindset.

Individuals with a fixed mindset may be less responsive to motivation than those with a growth mindset. This is because a fixed mindset can lead individuals to believe that their abilities are fixed, regardless of their effort. As a result, they may be less likely to believe that their effort will lead to improved outcomes or increased success. Individuals with a fixed mindset may be more focused on the end result, rather than the process of achieving it. This can lead them to become discouraged or give up more easily. A fixed mindset can create a sense of learned helplessness. This can result in decreased motivation and persistence over time. It is important to note that individuals with a fixed mindset can still be motivated by extrinsic factors, such as rewards or praise. While this type of motivation may be effective in the short term, it may not lead to sustained motivation and personal growth over time. To develop a more growth-oriented mindset, individuals may need to focus on intrinsic motivation, such as a desire for self-improvement.

Resilience: Individuals with a growth mindset tend to be more resilient in the face of setbacks and failures. They may view setbacks as temporary and see failures as opportunities for growth, rather than evidence of their limitations. This resilience can help individuals bounce back from setbacks and stay optimistic about their future. They understand that failure is a natural part of the learning process. Individuals with a growth mindset tend to be more persistent in pursuing their goals, even in the face of adversity. They are willing to put in the effort and dedication necessary to achieve their goals. They are better equipped to handle challenges and setbacks and are more likely to emerge from these experiences with greater resilience and adaptability. This can lead to greater success and fulfilment in all areas of their lives, as they can approach challenges with a positive and growth-oriented mindset.

Individuals with a fixed mindset may have a more limited capacity for resilience than those with a growth mindset. This is because a fixed mindset is characterized by a belief that abilities and intelligence are fixed traits that cannot be changed. They may be less likely to bounce back from setbacks and failures. They may become discouraged or give up when faced with challenges they perceive as beyond their abilities. They may be less willing to take risks or try new things, fearing the potential for failure or exposure to their perceived limitations. This can result in decreased resilience and persistence over time, as individuals become more discouraged and less motivated to pursue their goals. However, it is important to note that individuals with a fixed mindset can still develop resilience over time, by cultivating a growth mindset and embracing challenges as opportunities for learning and growth. By focusing on the process of learning and self-improvement, rather than just the result, individuals with a fixed mindset can develop greater resilience and adaptability over time.

Learning: Individuals with a growth mindset tend to be more open to learning new things and seeking out new experiences. They may be more likely to take on challenging tasks or seek out feedback to improve their performance. This can lead to greater personal and professional development over time. Individuals with a growth mindset understand that learning is an ongoing process that requires effort and dedication and is committed to continuous improvement. Learning can help them develop new skills, expand their knowledge, and explore new areas of interest. They may seek out new experiences and opportunities for growth and are willing to take on new challenges and try new things. Learning is a key component of a growth mindset, as it helps individuals develop greater self-awareness, resilience, and adaptability. By embracing the process of learning and seeking out opportunities for growth and development, individuals with a growth mindset can achieve greater success and fulfilment in all areas of their lives.

For individuals with a fixed mindset, learning may be perceived as threatening or difficult, as it challenges their belief that their abilities are fixed and cannot be improved upon. This can lead them to avoid learning opportunities. While learning may initially be challenging for individuals with a fixed mindset, it can ultimately lead to personal growth and improved performance. By embracing new experiences and opportunities for growth, they can challenge their existing beliefs and assumptions, and develop new skills and competencies that can help them achieve greater success and fulfilment in all areas of their lives.

Risk-taking: Individuals with a growth mindset may be more willing to take risks and try new things, as they view failure as a natural part of the learning process. This can lead to greater innovation and creativity in the workplace, as well as greater success in sports and other competitive arenas. Risk-taking can be an important component of developing and maintaining a growth mindset. Individuals with a growth mindset are willing to learn from their mistakes to improve their performance in the future. By taking risks, they can push beyond their comfort zones and expand their capabilities. They may learn new skills, gain new experiences, and discover new opportunities for personal and professional growth. They are willing to embrace uncertainty and ambiguity and are not afraid to make mistakes or experience failure along the way. By taking calculated risks and being willing to learn from their experiences, individuals with a growth mindset can achieve greater success.

Individuals with a fixed mindset may be more hesitant to take risks than those with a growth mindset. This is because a fixed mindset is characterized by a belief that one's abilities and intelligence are fixed. A fixed mindset can create a sense of learned helplessness, where individuals may believe that their efforts will not lead to improved outcomes. They usually have a fear of failing by taking any risk and they do not want to look like a failure in front of others. This can result in decreased risk-taking and initiative over time. However, it is important to note that individuals with a fixed mindset can still learn to take risks with practice and exposure to new experiences. With the help of external factors, such as support from others or access to resources, individuals with a fixed mindset can learn to overcome their fears and embrace new challenges. By gradually building confidence and taking on new experiences, individuals with a fixed mindset can develop greater resilience and adaptability over time.

Perseverance: Individuals with a growth mindset tend to be more persistent in pursuing their goals and overcoming obstacles. They may be more likely to stick with a difficult task or project, rather than give up prematurely. Perseverance can help individuals with a growth mindset build confidence in their abilities and develop a stronger sense of self-efficacy. By sticking with challenging tasks and seeing them through to completion, they can develop a sense of accomplishment and mastery that can help them tackle even greater challenges in the future. Perseverance gives them the ability to persist through difficulties and setbacks, and to maintain a sense of motivation and determination in pursuing their goals. It allows individuals to maintain their focus, resilience, and dedication in pursuit of their goals. By persisting through challenges and setbacks, individuals with a growth mindset can learn from failures, overcome obstacles, and achieve greater success and fulfilment in all areas of their lives.

Individuals with a fixed mindset may be less likely to persevere in the face of challenges and setbacks. This is because a fixed mindset is characterised by a belief that one's abilities and intelligence are fixed, regardless of the amount of effort put in. They perceive these challenges as evidence of their limitations. They lack the ability to put effort again and again into the same goal as they think that they have already tried and failed. Once the failure word comes to their mind they stop immediately and give up. They fail to understand that perseverance is all about being persistent in your goals to achieve success.

Overall, mindset can have a profound impact on behaviour and actions in a variety of contexts. By cultivating a growth mindset and embracing challenges and opportunities for growth, individuals can develop greater resilience, motivation, and adaptability, leading to greater success and fulfilment in all aspects of their lives. People with fixed mindsets usually end up in some sort of depression in their elderly age which leads to sadness and an unhealthy lifestyle but people with growth mindsets end up very satisfied with their lives, which always leads to a healthy lifestyle.

Strategies for Developing a Growth Mindset

It is never about talent, education or intelligence, it is all about how your mindset approaches a challenge. If you have a growth mindset then it is highly likely that you will succeed but with a fixed mindset, you will only find excuses and end up failing. So, developing a growth mindset can be a powerful tool for achieving success in all areas of life.

Let's explore some strategies for developing a growth mindset:

1. Embrace challenges: Instead of avoiding challenges, embrace them as opportunities for growth and learning. Recognize that mistakes and failures are a natural part of the learning process.
2. Stay positive: Cultivate a positive attitude and focus on the potential for growth and improvement. Surround yourself with positive people who support your growth and development.
3. Develop a sense of purpose: Identify your goals and values, and align your actions with them. Having a sense of purpose can help you stay motivated and focused on your goals.

4. View setbacks as opportunities: Instead of giving up in the face of setbacks, view them as opportunities for learning and growth. Every setback teaches us the wrongs we did and it gives us the opportunity to fix those wrongs.

5. Practice self-compassion: Instead of being self-critical and judgmental, practice self-compassion and kindness towards yourself. It helps boost our positive energy which gives us the confidence to achieve our goals.

6. Focus on effort over outcome: Instead of focusing solely on the outcome of your actions, focus on the effort and hard work that goes into achieving your goals. Enjoy the journey of achieving your goals.

7. Seek out feedback: Instead of fearing feedback, seek it out as an opportunity for learning and growth. Ask for feedback from others, and use it to improve your skills and performance. Be open to constructive criticism and use it to identify areas for improvement.

8. Cultivate a love of learning: Instead of viewing learning as a chore, cultivate a love of learning and a curiosity about the world around you. Focus on the process of learning, rather than the result. Celebrate progress and improvement, rather than just achievement.

9. Practice self-reflection: Reflect on your experiences and learn from them. Identify what worked well and what didn't, and use that knowledge to improve your performance in the future.

10. Develop resilience: Learn to bounce back from setbacks and failures, and use them as opportunities for growth. Focus on your strengths and use them to overcome challenges.

By incorporating these strategies into your daily life, you can develop a growth mindset that will help you achieve greater success and fulfilment in all aspects of your life. By cultivating a growth mindset, individuals can develop greater resilience, motivation, and adaptability. Remember, developing a growth mindset is an ongoing process that requires patience, persistence, and dedication.

* * *

2

Cultivating a Positive Attitude

Explanation of Positive Attitude

A positive attitude refers to a mental and emotional state characterized by optimistic, constructive, and hopeful thoughts and feelings. It involves approaching life's challenges and experiences with a positive outlook, focusing on the good aspects rather than dwelling on the negative. It is the attitude that makes you think that everything is possible and everything will be fine. It is a belief that everything will turn out to be all right. It is a state of mind in which you always expect and envision favourable outcomes.

An attitude is an observable aspect of one's behaviour. Therefore, whether an individual has a positive attitude or not is dependent on how they interact with the world and how others perceive them. However, what others observe in an individual is often a reflection of their inner self. For instance, individuals with a positive attitude are often able to find the silver lining in challenging situations, demonstrate kindness towards others even when it is not reciprocated, and exhibit a zest for life by smiling and laughing.

People with a positive attitude tend to:

1. Believe in their abilities and strengths, which helps boost their self-confidence.
2. Focus on solutions and opportunities instead of problems and obstacles.
3. Exhibit resilience in the face of adversity, allowing them to bounce back from setbacks more quickly.
4. Cultivate a sense of gratitude for the things they have, fostering contentment and happiness.
5. Engage in positive self-talk, affirming their worth and potential.
6. Maintain a growth mindset, viewing challenges and change as opportunities for growth and improvement.
7. Foster positive relationships with others, contributing to a supportive and uplifting social network.
8. Embrace a sense of purpose and meaning in life.

Having a positive attitude does not mean ignoring or denying the existence of difficulties, but rather approaching them with a constructive and hopeful perspective. This mindset can lead to numerous benefits, including improved mental and physical health, better relationships, and increased overall well-being.

A few examples of the benefits that a positive attitude can bring to our lives include:

1. Improved mental health: A positive attitude can help us manage stress and anxiety, and promote greater feelings of happiness and

well-being. It can also help us cope with difficult situations and bounce back from setbacks and challenges.

2. Enhanced relationships: A positive attitude can help us build stronger and more fulfilling relationships with others. We can foster deeper connections and create a more supportive and positive social environment by approaching others with kindness, compassion, and a positive outlook.

3. Increased productivity: A positive attitude can also enhance our productivity and performance. By approaching tasks with a positive and enthusiastic mindset, we can increase our motivation and focus, and achieve greater levels of success and achievement.

4. Improved physical health: A positive attitude has also been linked to better physical health outcomes, such as lower rates of depression, improved cardiovascular health, and longer lifespan.

5. More opportunities: Finally, a positive attitude can help us attract more opportunities and experiences into our lives. By approaching challenges and opportunities with optimism and an open mind, we can create a more expansive and fulfilling life for ourselves.

A positive attitude can bring many benefits to our lives, including improved mental and physical health, better relationships, increased productivity, and more opportunities for growth and fulfilment.

Cultivating a Positive Attitude

Cultivating a positive attitude takes consistent effort and practice, but the benefits are worth the investment. Developing a positive attitude requires a shift in perspective towards life. It involves moving away from a focus on negative aspects and towards a greater appreciation of the positives. Practising gratitude and cultivating positive thinking can help facilitate this shift. With practice, these habits can become easier to incorporate into one's daily routine.

Here are some strategies to help you develop a more positive outlook:

1. Practice gratitude: Focus on the things you're thankful for. Keep a gratitude journal, where you write down three things you're grateful for each day.

2. Re-frame negative thoughts: When you catch yourself thinking negatively, try to re-frame the thought into a more positive light. Look for the silver lining or find a lesson to learn from the situation. Replace negative thoughts with positive affirmations and constructive thoughts.

3. Surround yourself with positivity: Spend time with positive people who uplift and inspire you. This also includes consuming positive media and engaging in activities that make you feel good.

4. Set realistic goals: Establish achievable, specific goals for yourself. Breaking them down into smaller steps will help you stay motivated and positive as you work towards them.

5. Practice self-compassion: Be kind to yourself and recognize that it's okay to make mistakes. Treat yourself as you would a friend in need of support.

6. Focus on your strengths: Acknowledge your unique abilities and accomplishments, and use them to empower and motivate yourself.

7. Maintain a healthy lifestyle: Exercise, eat well, and get enough sleep to support both your physical and mental well-being.

8. Embrace change: Develop a growth mindset and view change as an opportunity for growth and improvement.

9. Help others: Engaging in acts of kindness and service can boost your happiness and create a sense of purpose.

10. Practice mindfulness: Develop an awareness of the present moment through meditation, deep breathing exercises, or other mindfulness practices.
11. Be patient: Remember that cultivating a positive attitude takes time and effort. Be patient with yourself and celebrate small wins along the way.

By incorporating these strategies into your daily life, you can gradually develop a more positive attitude and enjoy the benefits it brings, including increased happiness, improved relationships, and greater overall well-being. It can also help you find joy and fulfilment in the present moment, rather than focusing on negative thoughts or worries.

Tips for dealing with setbacks and failures in a positive way

Dealing with setbacks and failures in a positive way can help you learn from these experiences and turn them into opportunities for growth. This is essential for personal growth and resilience.

Below are some suggestions for how to approach setbacks and failures in a positive manner:

1. Accept and acknowledge your emotions: Recognize that setbacks and failures are a natural part of life and can happen to anyone. Allow yourself to feel disappointed or upset, but don't dwell on these emotions for too long. Acknowledging your emotions is a healthy way to process the situation and move forward.
2. Practice self-compassion: Treat yourself kindly during challenging times, just as you would support a friend or loved one. Remind yourself that it's okay to make mistakes and that everyone experi-

ences setbacks and failures.

3. Re-frame your perspective: Instead of viewing the setback as a failure, consider it a learning opportunity, rather than as a reflection of your self-worth. Ask yourself what you can learn from the experience, and how you can use that knowledge to grow and improve. This mindset shift can help you stay motivated and maintain a positive attitude.

4. Analyze the situation objectively: Take a step back and assess the situation from a neutral perspective. Break down what led to the setback or failure, identifying any areas where you could have done things differently. This can help you develop a plan to avoid similar issues in the future.

5. Focus on what you can control: Rather than dwelling on factors outside of your control, concentrate on the aspects of the situation that you can influence. This can help you regain a sense of agency and empowerment. Focus on your strengths and remind yourself of your abilities and accomplishments, and leverage these strengths to overcome setbacks and continue moving forward.

6. Set realistic and achievable goals: Break down your goals into smaller, manageable steps and celebrate your progress along the way. This will help you stay focused and motivated as you work towards overcoming setbacks and achieving success.

7. Seek support: Reach out to friends, family, or a professional counsellor for encouragement and guidance. Sharing your experiences and feelings with others can help you gain new perspectives and feel less alone. A strong support network can be invaluable in helping you navigate setbacks and failures.

8. Cultivate resilience: Develop coping strategies to bounce back from setbacks more quickly. This can include practising mindfulness, maintaining a healthy lifestyle, and engaging in activities that bring you joy and relaxation.

9. Maintain a growth mindset: Embrace the idea that setbacks and failures are opportunities for growth and development. Keep learning from your experiences and applying that knowledge to future challenges.

10. Maintain a long-term perspective: Remind yourself that setbacks and failures are a natural part of life and personal growth. Keep your long-term goals and vision in mind to maintain motivation and perspective.

Prioritize your mental and physical well-being during challenging times. Engage in activities that bring you joy, stay connected with loved ones, and maintain healthy habits. Stay flexible and adaptable, be open to change and adapt your approach as needed. This can help you find new solutions and strategies for overcoming setbacks. Stay persistent and don't give up on your goals because of a setback or failure. Learn from the experience, adjust your approach, and keep moving forward. You can develop a positive and resilient mindset that allows you to grow and learn from life's challenges. Practising this will help you stay positive in your life.

* * *

3

Overcoming Limiting Beliefs

Explanation of limiting beliefs and how they can hold us back from achieving our goals

L imiting beliefs are negative thoughts or beliefs that we hold about ourselves or the world around us. Such beliefs can be baseless self-criticisms that lead to negative outcomes. These beliefs can be rooted in past experiences, cultural conditioning, or other factors, and can often hold us back from achieving our goals and living our best lives.

Suppose, you have a limiting belief that you're not good at public speaking. As a result, you may turn down opportunities to speak to groups or feel anxious and fearful when presenting to an audience. Such preconceived notions can hold you back and limit your potential by preventing you from trying new things or pursuing new opportunities. This belief will make you struggle to take risks in your personal or professional lives. You will avoid challenges or opportunities for growth and give up easily.

Similarly, someone with a limiting belief that success is impossible may struggle to set and achieve goals, as they may not believe that their efforts will lead to meaningful results. They may lack motivation and drive and may feel resigned to a life of mediocrity or unfulfillment.

In both cases, these limiting beliefs can hold us back from achieving our full potential and living our best lives. They can prevent us from taking risks, pursuing our passions, and embracing new experiences and opportunities. They can also contribute to feelings of anxiety, depression, and low self-esteem, which can further hinder our ability to thrive.

Let's discuss the top five examples of limiting beliefs:

1. "I'm not good enough." - This belief can manifest in many areas of life, from personal relationships to career aspirations. It can prevent individuals from pursuing their goals or seeking out new opportunities.
2. "I'll never be able to change." - This belief can lead individuals to feel stuck or hopeless, as they believe that their current circumstances are permanent and cannot be altered. It can prevent them from making positive changes in their lives.
3. "Success is only for the lucky and talented." - This belief can lead individuals to feel discouraged or intimidated by the prospect of pursuing their goals. It can prevent them from working hard or taking risks, as they assume that success is outside of their control.
4. "I'm too old/young to do that." - This belief can limit individuals' sense of what is possible or achievable, based on their age. It can prevent them from pursuing new interests or taking on new

challenges.

5. "I don't deserve happiness/success." - This belief can lead individuals to feel unworthy of positive outcomes, such as happiness or success. It can prevent them from pursuing their goals or caring for themselves, as they do not believe they deserve good things.

By identifying and challenging our limiting beliefs, we can break free from these negative thought patterns and achieve greater success and fulfilment in our lives. This can involve re-framing negative self-talk, questioning the evidence behind our beliefs, and taking deliberate steps towards our goals, even in the face of uncertainty or risk. By developing a growth mindset and cultivating a positive and empowering belief system, we can overcome our limiting beliefs and achieve our full potential.

Strategies for identifying and overcoming limiting beliefs

Limiting beliefs can arise from various factors, but they typically stem from a common source: the brain's desire to shield oneself from future pain. Fear, impostor syndrome, and past experiences are some of the triggers that can cause limiting beliefs. These beliefs often originate in childhood and continue to evolve and shape over time as individuals encounter new experiences.

Limiting beliefs can obstruct the formation of positive beliefs by hindering personal growth and progress. Understanding the root cause of these beliefs can help individuals manage and overcome them by identifying the thought processes behind them. Identifying limiting beliefs is an important step in overcoming them and achieving success.

Here are some strategies for identifying limiting beliefs:

1. Pay attention to negative self-talk: Negative self-talk often reflects limiting beliefs. If you find yourself saying things like "I'm not good enough" or "I'll never be able to do that," it may be a sign of a limiting belief.
2. Identify patterns of behaviour: If you consistently avoid certain activities or situations, it may be because of a limiting belief. For example, if you avoid public speaking because you believe you are not good at it, that may be a limiting belief.
3. Look at past experiences: Past experiences can shape our beliefs about ourselves and our abilities. If you have had negative experiences in the past that are influencing your current beliefs, it may be a sign of a limiting belief.
4. Challenge assumptions: Sometimes we hold onto beliefs without really examining them. Take some time to challenge the assumptions you have about yourself and your abilities.
5. Seek feedback: Asking for feedback from trusted friends, family members, or colleagues can help you identify patterns of behaviour or beliefs that may be holding you back.

Identifying limiting beliefs is a process of self-reflection and self-awareness. By paying attention to our thoughts, behaviours, and past experiences, we can begin to uncover the beliefs that are holding us back and take steps to overcome them.

A limiting belief refers to a belief or mental state that imposes restrictions on oneself. These beliefs can impact an individual's ability to reach their full potential. While limiting beliefs are common, recognising and identifying them can enable proactive measures to prevent their effects. Such beliefs often originate from a negative or fearful mindset, which can hinder individuals from exploring new opportunities. Overcoming limiting beliefs is an important step in achieving success and fulfilment in life. This is a slow process but fruitful.

Follow these strategies for overcoming limiting beliefs:

1. Make a journal of beliefs: Usually, these beliefs are just negative thoughts in our brains instead of words. Write these thoughts down in your journal and you will see how untrue these thoughts are. It will be easy for you to separate facts and fiction.
2. Challenge your beliefs: One of the most effective ways to overcome limiting beliefs is to challenge them directly. Ask yourself whether your beliefs are based on facts or assumptions, and look for evidence that contradicts your beliefs.
3. Re-frame negative self-talk: Negative self-talk can reinforce limiting beliefs. Practice re-framing negative thoughts into more positive and empowering statements.
4. Practice self-compassion: Self-compassion involves treating your-self with kindness and understanding, even when you make mistakes or face setbacks. This can help you to develop a more positive self-image and overcome limiting beliefs.
5. Take action: Sometimes the best way to overcome limiting beliefs is to take action and prove to yourself that you are capable of achieving your goals. Start with small, achievable steps and gradually build up to more challenging goals.
6. Seek support: Overcoming limiting beliefs can be challenging, and it is important to have a support system in place. Seek support from friends, family members, or a professional therapist or coach who can help you to stay motivated and overcome obstacles.

Overcoming limiting beliefs is a process that requires self-reflection, self-compassion, and a willingness to challenge assumptions and take action. By taking these steps, you can break free from negative thought patterns and achieve your full potential.

Examples of people who have overcome limiting beliefs to achieve success

Individuals who overcome limiting beliefs demonstrate resilience and a growth mindset. They are willing to challenge their beliefs and take steps to shift their thought patterns in a positive direction. These individuals understand that their beliefs do not define their capabilities or potential and actively seek out opportunities to prove themselves wrong. They are open to learning and willing to take risks, even in the face of potential failure.

People who overcome limiting beliefs also tend to have a strong sense of self-awareness. They are able to recognize when their beliefs are holding them back and take steps to change their mindset. They may seek support from others, such as a mentor or therapist, to help them overcome their limiting beliefs.

Ultimately, those who overcome limiting beliefs are able to break free from the negative thought patterns that hold them back and unlock their full potential. They are able to pursue their goals with confidence and achieve success in all areas of their lives. There are so many individuals who have overcome limiting beliefs to achieve success in their lives. Here are a few examples:

Oprah Winfrey: Oprah Winfrey is a famous media personality and philanthropist who has faced a number of challenges and obstacles in her life, including poverty, abuse, and discrimination. Despite these challenges, she has been able to achieve incredible success and impact through her work in the media and her philanthropic endeavours. One of the limiting beliefs that Oprah faced early in her life was the belief that she was not good enough or worthy of success. As a child, Oprah experienced poverty, abuse, and other traumas, which led her to develop low self-esteem and a sense of unworthiness. She also faced discrimination and racism as a Black woman growing up in the United States in the 1950s and 60s, which further reinforced her sense of inferiority.

However, Oprah was able to overcome these limiting beliefs through a combination of hard work, perseverance, and a commitment to personal growth and development. She credits her success to her ability to embrace her vulnerability, be authentic, and face her fears head-on. One key turning point in Oprah's life was when she began to work on her inner self through therapy and personal development work. She also began to surround herself with positive and supportive people who encouraged her to pursue her dreams and believe in herself. Oprah also credits her success to her ability to focus on her strengths rather than her weaknesses. She recognized that she had a talent for connecting with people and sharing stories, and she was able to leverage that talent to build a successful career in media.

J.K. Rowling: J.K. Rowling is a famous author best known for her Harry Potter series of books. She faced a number of challenges and obstacles in her life before achieving success, including poverty, depression, and rejection from publishers. However, she was able to overcome these limiting beliefs and achieve great success through a combination of hard work, perseverance, and a commitment to her creative vision.

J.K. Rowling faced the belief that she was a failure. After graduating from college, Rowling struggled to find work and suffered from depression. She also experienced a number of personal setbacks, including the death of her mother and the breakdown of her first marriage. This led her to feel like a failure, both personally and professionally. However, Rowling was able to overcome this limiting belief by focusing on her zeal for writing and her commitment to her creative vision. She wrote the first Harry Potter book while she was struggling with depression and financial hardship, and was initially rejected by a number of publishers. However, she refused to give up on her vision and continued to work on the book until it was finally accepted for publication. Rowling also credits her success to her ability to embrace failure and rejection as part of the creative process. She recognized that rejection and setbacks were a natural part of the creative process and that she needed to keep working on her craft in order to achieve her goals.

Stephen Hawking: Stephen Hawking was a renowned physicist and author who made groundbreaking contributions to our understanding of the universe. Despite facing significant challenges throughout his life, including a diagnosis of ALS(Amyotrophic Lateral Sclerosis) that left him paralyzed and unable to speak, Hawking was able to achieve remarkable success and impact through his work in the field of physics.

In the early days of Hawking's life, he believed that he was not smart enough to pursue a career in physics. As a child, Hawking struggled with mathematics and was not a standout student in his early years. However, he was able to overcome this limiting belief by focusing on his strengths and developing a passion for physics. Hawking also faced a number of physical and health-related challenges throughout his life, including his diagnosis with ALS at the age of 21. This condition left him confined to a wheelchair and unable to speak without the use of a computerized voice synthesizer. Yet, he was able to overcome these physical limitations by developing innovative ways to communicate and continuing to work on his research despite his disability. Hawking's success is a testament to his ability to overcome limiting beliefs and persevere in the face of adversity. By focusing on his strengths, developing a passion for physics, and using his creativity to overcome physical limitations, he was able to achieve incredible success and impact in his field.

Malala Yousafzai: Malala Yousafzai is a well-known activist for women's education and human rights who has faced significant challenges and obstacles in her life. She grew up in the Swat Valley region of Pakistan, where the Taliban had banned girls from attending school. Despite this, Malala was determined to pursue her education and fight for the rights of girls and women in her community.

Malala faced many life-threatening challenges in her life which led her to believe that girls were not capable of achieving great things or of making a significant impact in the world. This belief was reinforced by the attitudes and practices of the Taliban and other conservative groups in her community, which sought to limit the education and opportunities available to girls and women. Yet, Malala was able to overcome this limiting belief by following her passion for education and her commitment to making a difference in the world. She began speaking out publicly about the importance of girls' education, even in the face of opposition and threats to her safety. In 2012, Malala was shot by a Taliban gunman while on her way to school. Despite this horrific act of violence, she refused to be silenced and continued to speak out about the importance of education and human rights. She went on to become the youngest-ever Nobel Prize laureate and has continued to be a powerful voice for change and social justice.

Jim Carrey: Jim Carrey is a well-known actor and comedian who has faced a number of challenges and obstacles in his life. He grew up in a low-income family in Canada and faced financial difficulties and personal struggles throughout his early career.

One of the limiting beliefs that Jim Carrey faced early in his life was the belief that he was not talented enough to succeed in show business. He struggled with self-doubt and insecurity and felt that his comedic talents were not appreciated by audiences or industry professionals. However, Carrey was able to overcome this limiting belief by focusing on his passion and his commitment to his craft. He continued to work on his comedy and acting skills and eventually landed roles in movies and television shows that showcased his unique talents and humour. Carrey also credits his success to his ability to embrace failure and rejection as part of the creative process. He recognized that setbacks and disappointments were a natural part of the entertainment industry and that he needed to keep working on his craft in order to achieve his goals. In addition to his work in show business, Carrey has also become a vocal advocate for mental health and wellness. He has spoken publicly about his struggles with depression and how he has used meditation and other practices to manage his mental health.

Bethany Hamilton: Bethany Hamilton is a professional surfer who has faced significant challenges and obstacles in her life. At the age of 13, she lost her left arm in a shark attack while surfing off the coast of Hawaii. Despite this traumatic event, Hamilton was able to overcome her limiting beliefs and become one of the most successful and inspiring surfers in the world.

Hamilton, after her tragic accident, believed that she would never be able to surf again. She struggled with feelings of fear, doubt, and insecurity, and was unsure if she would be able to adapt to surfing with just one arm. Hamilton was able to overcome these limiting beliefs by focusing on her zeal for surfing and her determination to succeed. She began practising and training with a new sense of purpose, and eventually returned to competitive surfing just a year after her accident. Hamilton also credits her success to her faith and her positive mindset. She has spoken publicly about the importance of staying focused, positive, and grateful in the face of challenges and setbacks, and has used her platform to inspire others to pursue their dreams and overcome their own limiting beliefs.

Elon Musk: Elon Musk is a well-known entrepreneur and visionary who has founded several successful companies, including Tesla, SpaceX, and PayPal. Despite his incredible success, Musk has faced a number of challenges and obstacles throughout his career, including financial difficulties, personal setbacks, and a number of high-profile failures.

Elon Musk has faced the limiting belief that some of his ambitious goals and ideas are impossible or too difficult to achieve. Musk has always been driven by a desire to push the boundaries of what is possible and has often been met with scepticism and doubt from critics and sceptics. However, Musk has been able to overcome these limiting beliefs by staying focused on his vision and his passion for innovation. He has a relentless work ethic and an unwavering commitment to his goals and has often worked tirelessly to overcome obstacles and setbacks. Musk also credits his success to his ability to embrace failure and learn from his mistakes. He has faced a number of high-profile failures throughout his career, including the failure of his first rocket launch at SpaceX and the production challenges at Tesla. However, he has always used these failures as opportunities for growth and learning and has used his experiences to refine his approach and develop new strategies for success.

Walt Disney: Walt Disney was a visionary filmmaker and entrepreneur who created some of the most iconic characters and stories in the history of entertainment. Despite his incredible success, Disney faced a number of challenges and obstacles throughout his life, including financial difficulties, personal setbacks, and rejection from critics and investors.

One of the limiting beliefs that Disney faced early in his career was the belief that he was not talented enough to succeed in the entertainment industry. As a young artist and filmmaker, Disney struggled to find work and to get his ideas and projects off the ground. However, Disney was able to overcome these limiting beliefs by focusing on his passion and his commitment to his vision. He continued to work on his art and his film-making skills, and eventually landed a job as a commercial artist, where he honed his skills and developed new techniques. Disney also credits his success to his ability to dream big and pursue his creative vision, even in the face of rejection and criticism. He was often met with scepticism and doubt from investors and industry professionals, but he refused to give up on his vision and continued to work tirelessly to bring his ideas to life.

Maya Angelou: Maya Angelou was a renowned poet, author, and civil rights activist who overcame significant challenges and obstacles in her life. She faced racism, poverty, and abuse throughout her childhood and adolescence, and struggled with feelings of self-doubt and insecurity for much of her life.

One of the limiting beliefs that Angelou faced early in her life was the belief that she was not worthy of love or respect. She had been abused as a child and felt like she was not deserving of kindness or affection from others. However, Angelou was able to overcome these limiting beliefs by developing a strong sense of self-worth and self-love. She began writing poetry and literature as a way to express her emotions and to find a sense of purpose and meaning in her life. Angelou also credits her success to her ability to face her fears and take risks, even when it was uncomfortable or difficult. She was an active participant in the civil rights movement, and often put herself in dangerous situations to fight for justice and equality.

Richard Branson: Richard Branson is a well-known entrepreneur and businessman who has founded several successful companies, including Virgin Group, Virgin Atlantic, and Virgin Mobile. Despite his incredible success, Branson has faced a number of challenges and setbacks throughout his career, including financial difficulties, personal setbacks, and negative feedback from investors and industry professionals.

One of the limiting beliefs that Branson faced early in his life was the belief that he was not a good student and did not have the necessary skills or knowledge to succeed in business. He struggled with dyslexia and found traditional academic settings challenging and frustrating. However, Branson was able to overcome these limiting beliefs by focusing on his strengths and his unique abilities. He recognized that he had a talent for entrepreneurship and innovation, and began pursuing his passion for business at a young age. Branson also credits his success to his ability to take risks and embrace failure. He has launched several ventures that have failed or struggled in the early stages, but he has always used these setbacks as opportunities for growth and learning and has used his experiences to refine his approach and develop new strategies for success.

Helen Keller: Helen Keller was a remarkable woman who overcame significant challenges and obstacles in her life. She was born deaf and blind and struggled to communicate with others and learn in traditional academic settings.

Helen Keller believed that she was incapable of learning or achieving success. She had been deaf and blind since infancy and had never experienced the world in the same way as her peers. However, Keller was able to overcome these limiting beliefs with the help of her teacher and mentor, Anne Sullivan. Sullivan was able to teach Keller how to communicate through a series of tactile signs and symbols and to introduce her to new concepts and ideas. Keller also developed a strong sense of resilience and determination and refused to give up on her dreams despite the challenges she faced. She went on to become a successful author and activist and dedicated her life to advocating for the rights of people with disabilities.

Michael Jordan: Michael Jordan is widely regarded as one of the greatest basketball players of all time. However, even he faced challenges and setbacks throughout his career, including negative feedback from coaches and doubts about his abilities.

One of the limiting beliefs that Jordan faced early in his career was the belief that he was not a good enough player. He was cut from his high school basketball team as a sophomore, which caused him to doubt his abilities and his future in the sport. However, Jordan was able to overcome these limiting beliefs by focusing on his passion and his commitment to improving his skills. He worked tirelessly to develop his basketball abilities and to prove his critics wrong and eventually went on to become a dominant player at both the college and professional levels. Jordan also credits his success to his ability to stay focused and motivated, even in the face of setbacks and challenges. He was known for his fierce competitiveness and his refusal to back down from a challenge, which helped him to succeed on and off the court.

Albert Einstein: Albert Einstein's limiting beliefs were largely imposed upon him by others during his early life. He faced several challenges and setbacks that could have made him doubt his own abilities:

1. Late development: Einstein didn't speak fluently until around age 4, which led his parents and others to worry about his intellectual abilities. This could have created a limiting belief that he was slow

or incapable of achieving great things.

2. Difficulty in school: Einstein struggled with the rigid educational system and authority figures, which led to conflicts with his teachers. They often criticized him for his independent thinking and nonconformity, potentially creating the limiting belief that he was a problematic student or couldn't succeed academically.

3. Rejection from academia: After graduating, Einstein was unable to secure a teaching position at a university, which may have contributed to self-doubt and limiting beliefs about his career prospects in academia.

Despite these challenges, Einstein overcame his limiting beliefs through the following approaches:

1. Intellectual curiosity: Einstein had an insatiable curiosity and desire to understand the world around him. He didn't let others' opinions dictate his passion for learning and discovering new ideas.

2. Persistence and resilience: Einstein's determination to pursue his interests and ideas, even in the face of setbacks and failures, helped him overcome the limiting beliefs that he faced.

3. Independent thinking: Rather than conforming to the expectations and norms of the educational system, Einstein embraced his own unique way of thinking and problem-solving. This allowed him to develop groundbreaking theories that revolutionized our understanding of the universe.

4. Support from mentors and peers: Throughout his life, Einstein found encouragement and support from individuals who recognized his potentials, such as his friend and fellow physicist Marcel Grossmann, who helped him secure a position at the Swiss Patent Office. This support allowed him to continue pursuing his ideas and eventually achieve widespread recognition for his work.

By maintaining his curiosity, resilience, and independent thinking, as well as finding support from others, Einstein was able to overcome his limiting beliefs and become one of the most renowned physicists in history.

One of the most common beliefs in the success stories of these individuals is the importance of having a growth mindset. All of the individuals we have discussed, from Maya Angelou to Michael Jordan to Richard Branson, faced significant challenges and obstacles throughout their lives and careers. However, they were all able to overcome these challenges by adopting a growth mindset, which emphasizes the importance of hard work, persistence, a willingness to learn from failure, embracing vulnerability, committing to personal growth and development, and focusing on strengths.

Another common belief in these success stories is the importance of staying focused on our passion and our goals. Each of these individuals was driven by a deep sense of purpose and a commitment to their vision, which helped them to overcome setbacks and to stay motivated in the face of adversity.

Overall, what we can learn from these success stories is that a positive mindset, a strong sense of purpose, and a commitment to learning and growth are essential for achieving success and impact in life. Developing resilience, working with supportive mentors, developing a strong sense of self-worth, refusing to be silenced by fear or intimidation, and using our creativity and perseverance to overcome obstacles are all major factors that contribute to adapting to a positive mindset. By adopting these beliefs and by staying focused on our goals and our passion, we can break free from negative thought patterns and achieve our full potential.

THE ART OF ATTITUDE

* * *

$$4$$

Building Resilience

Explanation of what resilience is and why it's important for success

A ccording to research, our level of resilience is influenced by various factors such as our personal characteristics, environmental factors, and the capacity for resilience that we develop through experience. Resilience is often perceived as the ability to recover quickly from adversity, which may be derived from its usage in the context of physical sciences. For instance, a material that can withstand being bent or stretched and then return to its original state is considered resilient. Examples could include a building that withstands strong winds or a plant that grows through tough soil. Likewise, resilience in the context of human experience can be defined as the ability to adapt our thoughts, emotions, and actions in the face of significant life disruptions or prolonged periods of stress, resulting in personal growth, enhanced wisdom, and improved abilities.

Resilience involves more than just bouncing back from adversity. Even for the most resilient individuals, sometimes it is very hard to return to the same state after a significant life event, such as the loss of a loved one or a serious medical diagnosis.

Psychology acknowledges that resilient individuals sometimes find better paths rather than recovering effortlessly. These challenging times can lead to personal growth and development, including

1. A better self-image: Resilient individuals discover unexpected abilities as they face new challenges.
2. Enhanced relationships: During tough times, resilient individuals prioritise positive relationships and recognize those who offer support.
3. Altered precedence: Resilience can provide a new perspective and help individuals clarify their values, life goals, and priorities.

Furthermore, a renewed sense of purpose can strengthen the resolve of already resilient individuals. Studies suggest that having a clear and meaningful purpose, and fully committing to a mission, can significantly enhance resilience.

Resilience is a multifaceted psychological trait that enables individuals to effectively cope with adversity, navigate through challenges, and recover from setbacks. It is a dynamic process that involves a combination of personal qualities, skills and behaviours that allows people to bounce back from difficult situations and adapt to change. The concept of resilience is deeply rooted in human nature, as it is an essential aspect of survival and growth just like persistence. Persistence is what keeps you going through difficulties and challenges meanwhile resilience is what makes you get back on track when you get sidetracked.

Resilience and Persistence Similarities

Resilience and persistence are closely connected because they both involve the ability to adapt and overcome challenges. Resilience is the ability to adapt and cope with adversity, stress, and challenging life events, while persistence is the ability to keep going despite setbacks and obstacles.

When faced with a challenge or setback, individuals who are resilient are better able to cope with the situation and find ways to adapt and bounce back. They may experience emotions such as disappointment, frustration, or sadness, but they are able to manage these emotions and stay focused on their goals. Resilient individuals are able to learn from their mistakes, adjust their approach, and persist in the face of difficulty.

Similarly, individuals who are persistent are often more resilient because they are able to maintain their focus and motivation even when things get tough. They are able to stay committed to their goals, even when faced with setbacks or obstacles. Persistent individuals are often able to draw on their inner strength and determination to overcome challenges and achieve their objectives.

Together, resilience and persistence form a powerful combination that can help individuals achieve their goals, overcome challenges, and navigate the ups and downs of life. By developing both resilience and persistence, individuals can build the skills and mindset needed to succeed in all areas of life.

Factors contributing to resilience

1. Emotional regulation: Resilient individuals can manage and regulate their emotions effectively, even in the face of adversity. They are able to recognize and accept their feelings, express them in healthy ways, and maintain emotional balance.

2. Optimism: A positive outlook on life, accompanied by hope and confidence in the future, is a crucial element of resilience. Optimistic individuals are more likely to seek solutions to problems, maintain motivation, and persevere in challenging situations.

3. Self-efficacy: Believing in one's own abilities to overcome obstacles and achieve desired outcomes fosters resilience. People with high self-efficacy are more likely to take initiative, set realistic goals, and maintain a sense of control over their lives.

4. Adaptability: The ability to adapt to change and navigate through uncertainty is a core aspect of resilience. Adaptable individuals can adjust their strategies, beliefs, or behaviours in response to new information or changing circumstances, allowing them to overcome challenges and thrive.

5. Problem-solving skills: Resilient people can effectively analyse problems, generate potential solutions, and implement appropriate strategies to address challenges. Effective problem-solving involves creative thinking, critical analysis, and persistence in the face of obstacles.

6. Support systems: A strong network of supportive relationships, including family, friends, and community members, can significantly enhance resilience. Social support provides emotional encouragement, practical assistance, and a sense of belonging, which can buffer against stress and promote well-being.

7. Sense of purpose: Having a clear sense of purpose, values, and

meaning in life can contribute to resilience by providing a sense of direction and motivation during challenging times. A strong sense of purpose can help individuals maintain focus, prioritise goals, and stay committed to their values even in the face of adversity.

8. Coping strategies: Resilient individuals can employ a variety of coping strategies to manage stress and navigate through difficult situations. These strategies may include active problem-solving, seeking social support, engaging in healthy self-care practices, or utilising cognitive techniques, such as re-framing or acceptance.

9. Learning from experience: A willingness to learn from setbacks, failures, or mistakes is a key aspect of resilience. Resilient individuals can reflect on their experiences, identify areas for growth, and apply the lessons learned to future challenges.

10. Persistence and determination: Resilience involves a strong sense of determination and the ability to persevere in the face of challenges or setbacks. Persistent individuals can maintain motivation, focus, and effort even when confronted with obstacles or difficulties.

Importance of resilience

Resilience is important for success because it enables individuals to effectively cope with adversity, manage stress, solve problems, build self-confidence, promote personal growth, develop a growth mindset, nurture strong relationships, and maintain a sense of purpose. These qualities and skills are essential for navigating through challenges and setbacks, and ultimately achieving success in various aspects of life.

Here are a few reasons why resilience is important for success:

- Overcoming obstacles and setbacks: Life inevitably presents challenges and setbacks, both personally and professionally. Resilience enables individuals to effectively cope with these difficulties, learn from them, and bounce back stronger. This adaptability is crucial for success, as it allows people to continue moving forward despite obstacles.
- Managing stress: Resilience helps individuals manage stress more effectively, as they are better equipped to regulate their emotions, maintain a positive outlook, and employ healthy coping strategies. Reduced stress levels can lead to improved mental and physical well-being, which ultimately contributes to success.
- Enhancing problem-solving skills: Resilient individuals tend to be better problem solvers. They approach challenges with a solution-oriented mindset, using creative thinking and persistence to overcome difficulties. These problem-solving skills are invaluable in achieving success, as they enable individuals to navigate through complex situations and find effective solutions.
- Building self-confidence: Resilience fosters self-confidence by helping individuals recognize their own strengths and abilities. This increased self-efficacy leads to greater motivation, persistence, and determination, which are essential qualities for achieving success in any area of life.
- Promoting personal growth: Resilience enables individuals to learn from their experiences, including failures and setbacks. This willingness to embrace challenges as opportunities for growth and learning can lead to the development of new skills, competencies, and insights that contribute to success.
- Encouraging a growth mindset: Resilient individuals often possess a growth mindset, which is the belief that abilities and intelligence can be developed through hard work, dedication, and learning. This mindset fosters persistence, motivation, and adaptability, all

of which are important factors in achieving success.

- Nurturing strong relationships: Resilience helps individuals develop and maintain strong, supportive relationships with family, friends, and colleagues. These connections can provide emotional, practical, and informational support during challenging times, which can contribute to success by bolstering well-being and providing resources for problem-solving and growth.
- Fostering a sense of purpose: Resilient individuals often have a strong sense of purpose, which can provide direction, motivation, and focus during challenging times. This sense of purpose can help individuals stay committed to their goals and values, even in the face of adversity, ultimately contributing to success.

Strategies for building resilience

Developing resilience is essential for navigating the ups and downs of life, maintaining good mental health, building confidence and self-esteem, enhancing relationships, and achieving personal goals. Resilience can be developed and enhanced over time through various strategies and interventions. Building resilience involves developing a variety of strategies that can help individuals effectively cope with adversity and enhance their overall ability to bounce back from challenges.

Here are some strategies for building resilience, including developing coping mechanisms, practising self-care, and cultivating a support network:

1. Develop healthy coping mechanisms: Learn to manage stress and navigate through difficult situations by employing a variety of healthy coping strategies, such as active problem-solving, seeking social support, engaging in self-care practices, and utilising cognitive techniques like re-framing or acceptance.

2. Practice self-care: Prioritise physical, emotional, and mental well-being by engaging in regular self-care activities. This can include maintaining a balanced diet, exercising regularly, getting sufficient sleep, practising relaxation techniques (e.g., mindfulness meditation, deep breathing exercises), and engaging in hobbies or activities that bring joy and satisfaction.

3. Cultivate a strong support network: Build and maintain strong social connections with family, friends, and community members who can provide emotional, practical, and informational support during challenging times. Nurture these relationships through regular communication, mutual trust, and empathy.

4. Enhance emotional intelligence: Learn to recognize, understand, and manage emotions effectively. Developing emotional intelligence can improve emotional regulation and contribute to resilience. Techniques such as mindfulness, journaling, and seeking feedback from trusted individuals can help in this area.

5. Foster optimism and hope: Encourage a positive outlook by focusing on the potential for growth and improvement, even in the face of adversity. Practice gratitude and seek out opportunities for personal growth and learning.

6. Set realistic goals and take action: Break down large goals into smaller, manageable steps, and take action towards achieving them. Monitor progress, celebrate accomplishments, and adjust goals as needed to maintain motivation and a sense of control.

7. Develop problem-solving skills: Cultivate the ability to effectively analyze problems, generate potential solutions, and implement

appropriate strategies to address challenges. Practise creative thinking, critical analysis, and persistence in the face of obstacles.

8. Embrace adaptability and flexibility: Learn to adapt to change and navigate through uncertainty by being open to new information and adjusting strategies, beliefs, or behaviours as needed. Develop a growth mindset that embraces challenges as opportunities for learning and growth.

9. Build self-efficacy: Strengthen confidence in your own abilities to overcome obstacles and achieve desired outcomes. Recognize and celebrate past successes, learn from setbacks, and seek out opportunities to develop new skills or competencies.

10. Find purpose and meaning: Identify your core values, passions, and goals to develop a clear sense of purpose and meaning in life. This can help provide direction and motivation during challenging times, enabling you to stay focused and committed to your values.

11. Learn from experience: Reflect on past experiences, including setbacks, failures, or mistakes, to identify areas for growth and apply the lessons learned to future challenges. This willingness to learn can help enhance resilience over time.

By incorporating these strategies into daily life and making a conscious effort to develop resilience, individuals can enhance their ability to effectively cope with adversity, maintain well-being, and recover from setbacks more quickly.

Examples of people who have demonstrated resilience in the face of challenges and adversity

You would not find any successful person who hasn't faced challenges in his or her life. As the saying goes," There is no easy mountain". So, everyone goes through some sort of difficulties in their life. Most people give up as they are missing the basic ingredients of being successful like passion, resilience and persistence. Resilience keeps you optimistic as when you bounce back from setbacks, you get a sense of positiveness which makes you believe that every problem has a solution, you just have to find the right angle to approach your problem.

There are many inspiring examples of individuals who have demonstrated resilience in the face of challenges and ultimately achieved success in their lives.

Here are a few notable examples:

1. **Abraham Lincoln**: Despite facing numerous personal and professional setbacks, including losing multiple elections and dealing with the death of his fiancée, Lincoln persevered and became the 16th President of the United States. He is widely regarded as one of the greatest presidents in American history, having led the country through the Civil War and contributed to the abolition of slavery.
2. **Nelson Mandela**: Mandela spent 27 years in prison for his fight against apartheid in South Africa. His resilience and determination allowed him to continue his struggle for racial equality even from behind bars. After his release, he played a crucial role in dismantling apartheid and went on to become the first black president of South Africa.
3. **Thomas Edison**: Edison faced numerous failures and setbacks

throughout his career as an inventor, including unsuccessful inventions and business ventures. However, his resilience and persistence led him to develop groundbreaking innovations such as the light bulb, phonograph, and motion picture camera.

4. **Stephen Hawking**: Diagnosed with Amyotrophic Lateral Sclerosis (ALS) at the age of 21, Hawking was given only a few years to live. Despite the debilitating effects of the disease, he continued his groundbreaking work in theoretical physics and cosmology, making significant contributions to our understanding of the universe.

5. **Helen Keller**: Despite being deaf and blind from a young age, Keller demonstrated remarkable resilience and determination. With the help of her teacher, Anne Sullivan, she learned to communicate and went on to become a renowned author, activist, and lecturer, advocating for people with disabilities.

6. **Steve Jobs**: After being forced out of the company he co-founded, Jobs demonstrated resilience by starting new ventures, including NeXT and Pixar Animation Studios. He eventually returned to Apple and led the company to unprecedented success with innovative products like the iPhone and iPad.

7. **Frida Kahlo**: Suffering from a debilitating accident and multiple health issues throughout her life, Kahlo channelled her pain and resilience into her artwork. Despite her physical challenges, she became one of the most celebrated artists of the 20th century.

8. **Viktor Frankl:** Frankl survived the Holocaust and went on to develop logotherapy, a form of psychotherapy focused on the search for meaning in life, and wrote the influential book "Man's Search for Meaning."

9. **Ludwig van Beethoven**: Beethoven faced numerous personal and professional challenges, including the loss of his hearing, but continued to compose some of his most famous and enduring

works.

10. **Mahatma Gandhi**: Gandhi faced numerous challenges, including imprisonment, while advocating for India's independence through nonviolent civil disobedience. His efforts ultimately led to India gaining independence from British rule.

11. **Marie Curie**: Curie overcame gender discrimination in the scientific community and personal tragedies to become the first woman to win a Nobel Prize and the only person to win Nobel Prizes in two different scientific fields.

12. **Harriet Tubman**: Born into slavery, Tubman escaped and went on to lead hundreds of enslaved people to freedom via the Underground Railroad, demonstrating immense bravery and resilience in the face of danger.

13. **Bill Gates**: Gates experienced early setbacks in his career, including the failure of his first business venture. However, he went on to co-found Microsoft, becoming one of the world's wealthiest and most influential entrepreneurs.

14. **Susan B. Anthony**: Despite facing ridicule, discrimination, and even arrest, Anthony persisted in her fight for women's rights and suffrage, playing a pivotal role in advancing women's rights in the United States.

15. **Christopher Reeve**: After a horse-riding accident left him paralyzed, the former Superman actor became an advocate for spinal cord injury research and disability rights, raising millions of dollars for medical research and increasing awareness about paralysis.

These examples highlight the power of resilience in overcoming adversity and achieving success across various fields, inspiring others to persevere in the face of challenges and setbacks.

BUILDING RESILIENCE

* * *

51

5

The Growth Mindset

Explanation of what the growth mindset is and how it differs from a fixed mindset

A growth mindset is a belief that an individual's abilities, intelligence, and talents can be developed and improved over time through effort, learning, and persistence. This concept, developed by psychologist Carol Dweck, stands in contrast to a fixed mindset, which is the belief that intelligence and abilities are static and unchangeable. The distinction between these two mindsets has significant implications for how people approach challenges, setbacks, and personal growth.

Individuals with a growth mindset see challenges as opportunities to learn and improve. They are more likely to embrace difficult tasks, believing that their efforts will lead to increased skills and knowledge. In the face of setbacks or failure, they persist and view these experiences as valuable learning opportunities. This mindset fosters a love of learning, a willingness to take risks, and a belief in the potential for personal growth and development.

On the other hand, individuals with a fixed mindset view their abilities and intelligence as inherent traits that cannot be changed. They are more likely to shy away from challenges, fearing that failure will expose their perceived lack of ability. When faced with setbacks, they may become defensive or give up, believing that their innate abilities are insufficient to overcome the challenge. This mindset can lead to a fear of failure, avoidance of risks, and resistance to learning and growth.

For example, Suppose someone wants to learn to play a musical instrument. If they have a fixed mindset, they may believe that they lack the natural talent or aptitude to become a musician. This belief can serve as an easy excuse to avoid practising since they assume that they will never be good at it. As a result, they may be less likely to take up the instrument or practice regularly.

On the other hand, someone with a growth mindset would be willing to try playing the instrument, even if they initially struggle or make mistakes. They would view mistakes and setbacks as opportunities for growth and learning, rather than as evidence of their innate limitations. They would practise regularly, seeking feedback and guidance, with the belief that hard work and effort can lead to improvement over time. As a result, they would be more likely to become skilled musicians and achieve their musical goals.

In a study conducted by Carol Dweck and her colleagues, the brains of individuals with different mindsets were analyzed. The researchers found that those with a fixed mindset exhibited heightened brain activity when informed of the correctness or incorrectness of their responses to a set of questions. These individuals were deeply invested in determining whether they had succeeded or failed. However, when offered assistance to learn from their mistakes, they displayed no interest. This was likely because they believed that improvement was not possible. They did not attempt to learn from their errors. Instead, they just focused on the outcome of the test.

The impact of these mindsets on various aspects of life, including academic achievement, personal growth and professional success, is profound. Research has shown that individuals with a growth mindset are more likely to persevere in the face of challenges, achieve higher levels of success, and maintain a more positive outlook on life.

- Academic achievement: In educational settings, a growth mindset has been linked to better academic performance, as students with this mindset are more likely to engage in effective learning strategies, such as seeking feedback, asking questions, and experimenting with different approaches to problem-solving. These students also tend to be more persistent in the face of academic challenges, viewing setbacks as opportunities to learn rather than as evidence of their inability.
- Personal growth: A growth mindset fosters a commitment to personal development and self-improvement. Individuals with this mindset are more likely to seek out new experiences, pursue their passions, and take risks in the service of their growth. They are also more likely to learn from their mistakes and setbacks, using these experiences as fuel for their ongoing development.
- Professional success: In the workplace, a growth mindset has been associated with greater motivation, productivity, and innovation. Employees with a growth mindset are more likely to embrace new challenges, take risks, and learn from their experiences. They are

also more likely to seek out feedback and collaborate effectively with colleagues, both of which contribute to their professional growth and success.

- Mental health and well-being: A growth mindset can also have positive effects on mental health and well-being. Individuals with this mindset are more likely to have higher self-esteem, as they view themselves as capable of growth and improvement. They are also more likely to exhibit resilience in the face of adversity, as they see challenges as opportunities to learn and grow rather than as threats to their self-worth.

Strategies for Cultivating a growth mindset

To cultivate a growth mindset, it is crucial to focus on the effort and the process rather than just the outcome. By emphasizing the effort, we encourage individuals to adopt a more positive attitude towards challenges and failure, which can lead to greater personal growth and development.

When individuals are praised solely for their accomplishments or the results they achieve, they may begin to feel that their abilities are fixed and unchangeable. This can lead to a fixed mindset, where individuals believe that their intelligence or talents are predetermined and cannot be improved upon. In contrast, when individuals are recognized for their efforts and progress, they are more likely to develop a growth mindset, where they believe that their abilities can be developed through hard work and dedication.

To appreciate the true effort, it is essential to celebrate the process of learning and development. This means emphasizing the importance of perseverance, grit, and resilience in the face of setbacks and challenges. Praising individuals for their effort, dedication, and persistence can encourage them to continue pushing themselves to achieve their goals, even when faced with adversity.

In addition, we should acknowledge and value the learning that takes place through mistakes and failures. When individuals are encouraged to learn from their mistakes, they are more likely to develop the resilience and adaptability needed to navigate life's challenges. By cultivating a growth mindset and celebrating the process of learning, we can help individuals develop the skills and mindset needed to thrive in today's rapidly changing world.

Cultivating a growth mindset involves developing an attitude and habits that support continuous learning, improvement, and resilience.
Here are some strategies to help you foster a growth mindset:

1. Embrace challenges: Welcome challenges as opportunities to grow. Approach difficult tasks with curiosity and enthusiasm, and be willing to take risks to achieve your goals. Seeing challenges as a natural part of the learning process helps you develop new skills and gain valuable experience.
2. Persist through obstacles: Persevere in the face of setbacks, obstacles, and failures. Recognize that setbacks are normal and that they provide opportunities to learn, adjust, and try again. Maintain a positive attitude and keep pushing forward, even when things get tough.
3. Learn from feedback: Actively seek feedback from others and use it to improve your skills and understanding. Be open to

constructive criticism and use it as a tool for growth. Reflect on your experiences, consider alternative perspectives, and integrate new information into your approach.

4. Focus on effort and progress: Value effort and persistence, and recognize that learning and growth require hard work and dedication. Praise yourself and others for the effort put into tasks, rather than focusing solely on the outcomes. Monitor your progress and celebrate small victories along the way.

5. Cultivate curiosity and a love of learning: Develop a genuine interest in learning new things and exploring new ideas. Engage in activities that challenge and expand your knowledge, and be open to acquiring new skills and understanding. Embrace lifelong learning as a path to personal and professional growth.

6. Re-frame setbacks and failures: Instead of viewing setbacks and failures as evidence of your limitations, see them as valuable learning opportunities. Reflect on what went wrong, identify areas for improvement, and use this information to adapt and grow.

7. Develop a flexible and adaptive mindset: Be willing to change your approach and strategies when faced with new information or circumstances. Stay open to new ideas and perspectives, and be prepared to adjust your plans and goals as needed.

8. Surround yourself with growth-minded individuals: Seek out people who share your passion for learning and growth. Support and encourage each other to take on challenges, persist through obstacles and learn from experiences. Engage in open and constructive discussions to exchange ideas and insights.

9. Set realistic yet challenging goals: Establish goals that are achievable yet challenging, providing a sense of purpose and direction. Break down large goals into smaller ones, manageable steps, and focus on the process of growth and development rather than solely on the end result.

10. Practice self-compassion: Be kind to yourself when you face setbacks or failures. Acknowledge that everyone makes mistakes and encounters challenges, and use these experiences as opportunities to learn and grow. Treat yourself with understanding and encouragement, just as you would a friend or loved one.

By incorporating these strategies into your daily life and consciously cultivating a growth mindset, you will be better equipped to face challenges, learn from setbacks, and achieve greater personal and professional success. Meditation can be a powerful tool for developing a growth mindset by increasing self-awareness, reducing stress and anxiety, improving focus and concentration, increasing resilience, and promoting self-compassion.

Examples of people who have used a growth mindset to achieve success

All successful people have a growth mindset. There are so many examples of people who used their growth mindset to achieve success. We already discussed a few of them in our last chapters.

Here are ten more additional examples of individuals who have used a growth mindset to achieve success in various fields:

1. Dr Carol Dweck: The psychologist who developed the concept of growth mindset, Dweck has used her research and findings to help people develop more effective learning strategies and achieve greater success in various aspects of life.
2. Stephen King: The renowned author faced numerous rejections before publishing his first novel, "Carrie." King's growth mindset

and persistence in the face of rejection ultimately led to a successful career as a prolific writer.

3. Arianna Huffington: The co-founder of The Huffington Post experienced setbacks, including a failed political campaign and a poorly received book, before achieving success as an entrepreneur and author. Her growth mindset enabled her to learn from these experiences and build a successful media company.

4. Sara Blakely: Blakely, the founder of Spanx, faced numerous rejections from manufacturers when trying to launch her revolutionary shapewear line. With a growth mindset, she persevered, eventually turning Spanx into a billion-dollar business.

5. Fred Astaire: The iconic dancer and actor faced early criticism and rejection, with one early report stating he "can't act" and "can't sing." With a growth mindset, Astaire persevered, becoming one of the most influential dancers and performers in the entertainment industry.

6. Ursula Burns: Rising from a challenging upbringing in a low-income neighbourhood, Burns joined Xerox as an intern and eventually became the company's first African American woman CEO. Her growth mindset allowed her to break barriers and achieve success in the corporate world.

7. Colonel Harland Sanders: The founder of Kentucky Fried Chicken (KFC) faced numerous setbacks, including failed businesses and over a thousand rejections from investors, before establishing the successful fast-food chain. Sanders' growth mindset and persistence ultimately led to his success as an entrepreneur.

8. Sylvia Plath: Despite battling mental health issues and facing rejection from publishers, Plath became one of the most influential poets of the 20th century. Her growth mindset allowed her to use her experiences and challenges as inspiration for her work.

9. Jack Ma: The Alibaba Group founder experienced several failures,

including being rejected from numerous jobs and facing setbacks in his early business ventures. By adopting a growth mindset, Ma overcame these challenges and built one of the world's largest e-commerce companies.

10. Reshma Saujani: The founder of Girls Who Code, Saujani started the nonprofit after a failed political campaign. Her growth mindset allowed her to pivot and create an organization dedicated to closing the gender gap in technology, impacting thousands of young women's lives.

These individuals exemplify the power of a growth mindset in overcoming adversity and achieving success across various fields. Their stories inspire others to adopt a growth mindset and work towards their own goals and aspirations.

* * *

6

Mindfulness and Meditation

Explanation of the benefits of mindfulness and meditation for improving focus, reducing stress and anxiety, and enhancing overall well-being

Mindfulness and meditation have gained widespread recognition and interest in recent years for their numerous benefits, including improved focus, reduced stress and anxiety, and enhanced overall well-being. This growing appreciation stems from a combination of scientific research and anecdotal evidence, highlighting the profound impact of these practices on our mental, emotional, and physical health.

Mindfulness is the practice of maintaining a non-judgmental awareness of our thoughts, feelings, bodily sensations, and surrounding environment in the present moment. It involves paying attention to our experiences as they unfold, without getting caught up in judgments, evaluations, or mental commentary. The goal is to cultivate an attitude of curiosity, openness, and acceptance towards our inner and outer experiences.

By developing mindfulness, we learn to be more fully present in our lives, rather than being constantly preoccupied with thoughts about the past or worries about the future. This heightened state of awareness allows us to engage with our experiences more deliberately and fully, leading to a greater sense of well-being, improved focus, and enhanced emotional regulation.

Mindfulness can be practised in everyday activities, such as eating, walking, or engaging in conversation, as well as through more formal meditation practices that specifically focus on cultivating present-moment awareness. The key is to approach our experiences with an open and non-judgmental attitude, allowing ourselves to observe and explore our thoughts, emotions, and sensations as they arise without becoming overwhelmed or consumed by them.

Meditation, on the other hand, is a mental practice or technique that involves focusing the mind and cultivating a state of relaxed concentration, inner calm, and heightened awareness. The ultimate goal of meditation varies depending on the specific tradition or practice, but common objectives include achieving mental clarity, emotional stability, self-awareness, and a more profound sense of well-being.

There are various different forms of meditation, each with its own set of techniques and approaches. Some common meditation practices include:

1. Concentration meditation: This form of meditation involves

focusing the mind on a single point of reference, such as the breath, a mantra, or a specific object. The goal is to train the mind to maintain attention on this singular focus, which can help improve concentration and mental clarity.

2. Mindfulness meditation: In mindfulness meditation, practitioners aim to cultivate a non-judgmental awareness of their thoughts, feelings, bodily sensations, and surrounding environment in the present moment. This practice helps develop present-moment awareness and can lead to greater emotional regulation and overall well-being.

3. Loving-kindness meditation (Metta meditation): This type of meditation focuses on developing feelings of love, kindness, and compassion for oneself and others. Practitioners typically repeat phrases or intentions aimed at cultivating these positive emotions, which can contribute to improved emotional well-being and interpersonal relationships.

4. Body scan meditation: This practice involves directing one's attention to different parts of the body sequentially, often starting from the feet and moving upwards. The goal is to cultivate an awareness of bodily sensations and promote relaxation and stress reduction.

5. Transcendental Meditation (TM): TM is a specific technique that involves silently repeating a personal mantra, typically for 15 to 20 minutes twice a day. This form of meditation promotes deep relaxation, reduced stress, and increased mental clarity.

6. Guided meditation: In guided meditation, a practitioner follows the instructions of a teacher or audio recording, which may involve visualization, body scans, or other techniques designed to promote relaxation and mindfulness.

While the specific methods and techniques may vary across different meditation practices, the underlying principle of training the mind to focus, cultivate awareness, and develop inner calm is consistent. Regular meditation practice has been shown to provide numerous benefits, including reduced stress and anxiety, improved focus and concentration, enhanced emotional well-being, and better overall physical health. By reducing stress and anxiety, individuals approach challenges with a more positive and growth-oriented mindset. Meditation can help individuals become more aware of their thoughts and beliefs. It helps individuals identify limiting beliefs and negative self-talk that may be holding them back. Increased focus and concentration help to stay present and to engage with better learning skills. Meditation can help individuals develop greater resilience by teaching them how to cope with difficult emotions and challenging situations. These are just a few of the benefits of meditation and mindfulness which help develop a growth mindset.

The benefits of mindfulness and meditation are manifold and can be observed across several dimensions of well-being, including cognitive, emotional, and physical health.

Let's dive into a few of the main benefits of meditation and mindfulness:

- Improved focus and concentration: One of the primary benefits of mindfulness and meditation is their ability to enhance our attentional capacities. By training the mind to remain focused on a single point of reference, such as the breath, a mantra, or the sensations of the body, we develop greater control over our attentional resources. This increased focus and concentration can significantly impact our daily lives, helping us stay on task, make fewer errors, and maintain a clear and alert mental state.
- Reduced stress and anxiety: Another well-documented benefit of

mindfulness and meditation is their capacity to alleviate stress and anxiety. These practices encourage us to adopt a non-reactive and accepting attitude towards our experiences, allowing us to navigate life's challenges with greater equanimity and resilience. By cultivating present-moment awareness, we can learn to disengage from the habitual patterns of worry, rumination, and negative self-talk that often exacerbate stress and anxiety.

- Enhanced emotional regulation: Mindfulness and meditation can also help us develop greater emotional intelligence and regulation. As we become more attuned to our inner experiences, we can gain a deeper understanding of our emotional triggers and patterns, allowing us to respond to life's ups and downs with greater skill and wisdom. Through the cultivation of self-awareness, self-compassion, and non-judgmental acceptance, we can learn to navigate our emotions with greater ease and grace.

- Improved physical health: The benefits of mindfulness and meditation extend beyond mental and emotional well-being to encompass physical health as well. Numerous studies have demonstrated the impact of these practices on reducing blood pressure, improving immune function, and alleviating chronic pain. Additionally, mindfulness and meditation have been shown to promote healthier sleep patterns, which can have a profound effect on overall health and well-being.

- Enhanced well-being and life satisfaction: Practicing mindfulness and meditation can contribute to a greater sense of overall well-being and life satisfaction. As we become more present and engaged with our experiences, we can derive greater joy and contentment from life's simple pleasures. Furthermore, mindfulness and meditation can help us cultivate a deeper sense of meaning, purpose, and connection, contributing to a more fulfilling and rewarding existence.

- Increased self-awareness and self-compassion: Mindfulness and meditation can help us develop a deeper understanding of ourselves, our thoughts, and our emotions. This self-awareness can lead to increased self-compassion, as we learn to treat ourselves with kindness and understanding, even in the face of personal shortcomings and failures. Self-compassion can contribute.

Strategies for practising mindfulness and meditation in daily life

As we discussed, Incorporating mindfulness and meditation into daily life can be highly beneficial for one's mental and emotional well-being. Practising mindfulness and meditation involves intentionally focusing your attention on the present moment, without judgment or distraction. Mindfulness and meditation can take many different forms but typically involve sitting or lying down in a comfortable position and focusing on your breath or a specific object, such as a candle or a sound. Mindful Breathing involves focusing on your breath and observing the sensations of each inhale and exhale. Bringing awareness to each part of your body, from your toes to the top of your head, noticing any sensations or tension.

During mindfulness and meditation, you may experience a range of sensations, thoughts, and emotions. The goal is to observe these experiences without judgment or attachment, simply noticing them and allowing them to pass. Cultivating feelings of kindness and compassion towards yourself and others.

Here are some strategies to help you practice mindfulness and meditation regularly:

1. Establish a routine: Set aside a specific time each day for your mindfulness or meditation practice. Having a consistent routine will make it easier to maintain your practice over time. Many people find it helpful to meditate in the morning, as it sets a positive tone for the day. However, you can choose a time that works best for you.

2. Start small: If you're new to meditation, begin with short sessions of around 5 to 10 minutes. Gradually increase the duration as you become more comfortable and familiar with the practice.

3. Create a dedicated space: Designate a quiet, comfortable space in your home for your meditation practice. Depending on your preferences and available space, this could be a small corner or an entire room. Having a dedicated meditation area can help reinforce your commitment to the practice.

4. Use guided meditation apps or recordings: To support your practice, consider using guided meditation apps or recordings, especially if you're new to meditation. These tools can help you learn various meditation techniques and maintain focus during your sessions.

5. Practice mindfulness throughout the day: Mindfulness can be incorporated into everyday activities, such as eating, walking, or engaging in conversation. To practice mindfulness in daily life, try to be fully present in each moment, paying attention to your thoughts, feelings, and bodily sensations without judgment.

6. Set an intention: Before each meditation or mindfulness session, set an intention for your practice. This can help you stay focused and provide a sense of purpose to your practice.

7. Use reminders: Use reminders or alarms on your phone or computer to prompt you to take brief mindfulness breaks throughout

the day. These short pauses can help you re-centre and refocus your attention on the present moment.

8. Join a meditation group or take a class: Engaging with a community of like-minded individuals can be a great source of support and motivation. Participating in a meditation group or taking a class can help you deepen your practice and learn from the experiences of others.

9. Be patient and gentle with yourself: Developing a consistent meditation and mindfulness practice takes time and patience. Be kind to yourself if you encounter challenges or experience lapses in your practice. Remember that progress may be gradual, and it's essential to maintain a non-judgmental and compassionate attitude towards yourself.

10. Keep a meditation journal: Tracking your meditation experiences can help you stay accountable and gain insights into your practice. Consider keeping a journal to document your thoughts, feelings, and observations after each session.

By incorporating these strategies into your daily life, you can establish a regular mindfulness and meditation practice that contributes to improved well-being, reduced stress, and enhanced focus and self-awareness. Remember that practising mindfulness and meditation is a skill that takes time and patience to develop. The key to mindfulness and meditation is to approach it with an open and curious mind, without judgment or expectation.

In addition to formal meditation practice, you can also practice mindfulness in your daily life by bringing greater awareness to your daily activities. For example, you can practice mindfulness while eating, walking, or engaging in other routine tasks. The goal is to focus your attention on the present moment and cultivate a greater sense of awareness and connection with your surroundings.

* * *

69

7

Strategies for Success

Practical Strategies for achieving success

To achieve something, first and foremost it's important to ask and answer yourself the further questions - What? Why? How and When? What is something that you want to achieve, why do you want to achieve it, and how and when do you want to achieve it? Everything needs a plan of action. So before talking about the practical strategies for success, we should focus on strategizing the steps we need to take to get where we want to go.

Strategising is crucial for achieving success as it helps individuals to identify and prioritize their goals, develop a plan of action, and make the most effective use of their resources and abilities. Without a strategy, individuals may lack direction and focus, leading to wasted effort, time, and resources. Achieving success often requires implementing practical strategies that can help you stay focused, organized, and motivated.

Set SMART Goals

Setting SMART goals can be an effective way to achieve success because it provides a clear framework for defining and working towards your goals. SMART is an acronym that stands for Specific, Measurable, Achievable, Relevant, and Time-Bound. Here's how each of these elements can help you achieve success:

1. Specific: Setting specific goals means that you have a clear idea of what you want to accomplish. Instead of setting a vague goal like "get in better shape," you might set a specific goal like "lose 10 pounds in the next 3 months."
2. Measurable: Measurable goals enable you to track your progress and know when you've achieved your goal. In the example above, you could measure your progress by tracking your weight loss each week.
3. Achievable: Setting achievable goals means that you're setting yourself up for success. It's important to set goals that are challenging, but also realistic and achievable based on your current skills and resources.
4. Relevant: Relevant goals are aligned with your values and priorities and are meaningful to you. When you set goals that are relevant, you're more likely to stay motivated and committed to achieving them.
5. Time-Bound: Setting a deadline for achieving your goal helps create a sense of urgency and keeps you accountable. In the example above, setting a goal of losing 10 pounds in 3 months provides a clear deadline to work towards.

By setting SMART goals, you can create a clear roadmap for achieving success. You'll have a specific, measurable, and achievable goal that is aligned with your values and priorities and has a clear deadline for completion. This helps you stay focused, motivated, and accountable, which can ultimately lead to greater success in achieving your goals.

Develop a plan of action

Developing a plan of action is critical for achieving success because it provides a roadmap for what steps need to be taken in order to reach a goal. Here are some key reasons why developing a plan of action is important:

1. Provides clarity: A plan of action provides clarity and structure for what needs to be done to achieve a goal. It breaks down a large goal into smaller, more manageable steps that are easier to follow and track progress.
2. Increases focus: A plan of action helps you focus on the specific steps needed to achieve a goal, rather than feeling overwhelmed by the bigger picture. This focus helps you prioritize and stay on track, avoiding distractions or getting sidetracked by unrelated tasks.
3. Boosts motivation: Having a clear plan of action can boost motivation by providing a sense of purpose and direction. It helps you visualize the end result and feel more confident in your ability to achieve the goal.
4. Encourages accountability: A plan of action helps to establish clear deadlines and milestones, making it easier to hold yourself accountable for progress. It also helps you identify potential obstacles or challenges that may arise and develop strategies to

overcome them.

5. Improves efficiency: A plan of action helps to streamline the process of achieving a goal by breaking it down into smaller, more manageable steps. This makes it easier to stay organized and focus on what needs to be done in a systematic and efficient way.

Developing a plan of action is crucial for achieving success because it provides clarity, focus, motivation, accountability, and efficiency. By breaking down a goal into smaller steps and creating a plan to achieve each one, you are more likely to reach your goal and experience a greater sense of accomplishment along the way.

Prioritize tasks

Prioritizing tasks is a critical aspect of achieving success because it allows you to focus your time and energy on the most important and impactful activities. Here are some key ways in which prioritizing tasks can help you achieve success:

1. Increases focus: Prioritizing tasks helps you to focus on the most important and urgent tasks, avoiding distractions and reducing the likelihood of wasting time on less important activities.
2. Saves time: By focusing on the most important tasks first, you can complete them efficiently and effectively, potentially freeing up time for other tasks or activities.
3. Reduces stress: Prioritizing tasks can reduce stress by helping you to feel more in control of your workload and ensuring that you are working on tasks that align with your goals and priorities.
4. Boosts productivity: By focusing on the most important tasks

and completing them efficiently, you can increase your overall productivity and accomplish more in less time.

5. Increases effectiveness: Prioritizing tasks can increase your effectiveness by ensuring that you are focusing on activities that will have the greatest impact on achieving your goals.

In order to prioritize tasks effectively, it's important to start by setting clear goals and identifying the tasks that are most critical to achieving those goals. You can then rank these tasks based on urgency, importance, or other relevant criteria, and create a plan to work through them in order of priority.

By prioritizing tasks effectively, you can work smarter, not harder, and achieve greater success in less time. You'll be able to focus your efforts on the activities that matter most and make steady progress towards your goals over time.

Develop positive habits

Developing positive habits is critical for achieving success because it helps to ensure that your actions are aligned with your goals and values. Here are some key reasons why developing positive habits is important:

1. Consistency: Developing positive habits helps you to consistently take action towards your goals, even when you don't feel motivated. Habits become automatic over time, making it easier to stick with them and make progress towards your goals.
2. Productivity: Positive habits can help you to be more productive by reducing decision fatigue and allowing you to focus your energy

on the tasks that matter most.

3. Self-discipline: Developing positive habits requires self-discipline, which is an essential trait for achieving success. By regularly practising self-discipline, you can develop the mental and emotional strength to overcome challenges and persevere through setbacks.

4. Mental and physical health: Many positive habits, such as exercise, healthy eating, and meditation, have been shown to improve both mental and physical health. By developing these habits, you can improve your overall well-being and increase your capacity for success.

5. Momentum: Developing positive habits can create momentum towards achieving your goals. By making progress each day, you build momentum and create a positive cycle of success.

To develop positive habits, it's important to start by setting clear goals and identifying the habits that will support those goals. Then, break those habits down into smaller, manageable steps and make a plan to work on them consistently over time. By tracking your progress and celebrating your successes along the way, you can build positive momentum and achieve greater success over time.

Establish a daily routine

Establishing a daily routine is important for achieving success because it provides structure and consistency, helping you to stay on track and make progress towards your goals. Here are some key ways in which establishing a daily routine can help you achieve success:

1. Increased productivity: Having a daily routine helps you to

prioritize your tasks and manage your time effectively, allowing you to be more productive and accomplish more each day.

2. Improved time management: By establishing a daily routine, you can allocate your time more effectively and ensure that you are making progress towards your goals each day.

3. Reduced stress: A daily routine can help to reduce stress by providing structure and predictability, reducing the need for decision-making and creating a sense of stability and control.

4. Increased motivation: A daily routine can help to increase motivation by creating a sense of purpose and direction. When you know what you need to do each day, you are more likely to feel motivated to do it.

5. Improved health and well-being: A daily routine can include activities that support your physical and mental health, such as exercise, meditation, healthy eating and sleeping on time, which can improve your overall well-being and increase your capacity for success.

To establish a daily routine, start by identifying your goals and the activities that will support those goals. Then, create a schedule that includes these activities, as well as time for work, leisure, and other responsibilities. Be sure to set realistic expectations and be flexible, as your routine may need to evolve over time to accommodate changes in your life or goals. By sticking to your routine and making adjustments as needed, you can create a structure that supports your success and helps you achieve your goals.

Monitor your progress

Monitoring your progress is essential for achieving success because it allows you to track your progress towards your goals, identify areas for improvement, and make necessary adjustments. Here are some key reasons why monitoring your progress is important:

1. Motivation: Monitoring your progress can help to keep you motivated by showing you how far you've come and reminding you of what you've accomplished so far. This can help you to stay focused and committed to your goals, even when progress is slow or setbacks occur.

2. Accountability: Monitoring your progress can help to hold you accountable for your goals and commitments. By regularly checking in on your progress, you can identify areas where you may be falling short and make adjustments to stay on track.

3. Feedback: Monitoring your progress can provide valuable feedback that can help you to identify areas for improvement and make necessary changes. This can help you to refine your approach and improve your chances of success.

4. Identify what's working: Monitoring your progress can help you to identify what is working well and what isn't, which can help you to refine your approach and optimize your efforts. By focusing on what is working, you can build on your strengths and increase your chances of success.

5. Course correction: Monitoring your progress can help you to identify when things are not working as planned and make necessary course corrections. This can help you to avoid wasting time and resources on strategies that are not effective and make the most of your efforts towards your goals.

To monitor your progress effectively, it's important to set clear and measurable goals, break them down into smaller milestones, and track your progress regularly. This can be done through regular check-ins, journaling, tracking apps, or other tools that work for you. By monitoring your progress, you can stay focused, motivated, and on track towards achieving your goals.

Learn from setbacks

Learning from setbacks is crucial for achieving success because setbacks are a natural part of the journey towards any goal. No matter how well we plan or prepare, setbacks and failures are bound to occur at some point. However, what distinguishes successful people is their ability to learn from setbacks and use them as opportunities for growth and improvement.

Here are some key reasons why learning from setbacks is important for achieving success:

1. Gain new insights: Setbacks can provide valuable feedback and insights that can help you to refine your approach and improve your chances of success. By learning from setbacks, you can identify what went wrong and why, and use this information to make necessary adjustments.

2. Build resilience: Setbacks can be discouraging and even demotivating, but by learning from them, you can build resilience and develop the mental and emotional fortitude needed to persevere in the face of challenges.

3. Adaptability: The ability to learn from setbacks and make adjustments is essential for adaptability, which is a key skill in

today's rapidly changing world. By developing this skill, you can become more flexible and better equipped to navigate unforeseen challenges.

4. Innovation: Learning from setbacks can also spark creativity and innovation, as it can inspire new ideas and approaches that may not have been considered before. By reflecting on what went wrong and what could have been done differently, you may be able to come up with new and innovative solutions that can help you to achieve your goals more effectively.

5. Increased confidence: When you learn from setbacks and overcome challenges, it can increase your confidence and self-efficacy, which can improve your performance and increase your chances of success.

Setbacks are a natural part of any journey towards success, but learning from them can provide valuable feedback and insights, build resilience, enhance adaptability and innovation, and increase confidence. By embracing setbacks as opportunities for growth and improvement, you can increase your chances of achieving success.

Seek feedback and support

Engage with mentors, peers, or professionals who can provide constructive feedback, guidance, and support. This input can help you gain new perspectives, improve your skills, and stay accountable. Seeking feedback and support is important for achieving success in a number of ways:

1. Identifying blind spots: Sometimes, we may not be aware of our

own limitations or areas for improvement. Seeking feedback from others can help to identify blind spots and provide insights into areas where we can grow and develop.

2. Gaining new perspectives: Seeking feedback and support from others can also provide new perspectives on our goals and challenges. Other people may have different experiences, skills, or perspectives that can help us to see things in a new light and come up with new solutions.

3. Building relationships: Seeking feedback and support can also help to build relationships with others who can provide guidance, mentorship, and support on our journey towards success. These relationships can be valuable sources of inspiration, motivation, and accountability.

4. Accountability: Seeking feedback and support can also help to provide accountability. When we share our goals and plans with others, we are more likely to follow through on them and stay committed to achieving them.

5. Continuous learning: Seeking feedback and support can also help to foster a mindset of continuous learning and improvement. By seeking feedback and support, we can continue to develop our skills, knowledge, and abilities, and ultimately become more successful.

Seeking feedback and support is important for achieving success because it can help us to identify blind spots, gain new perspectives, build relationships, provide accountability, and foster a mindset of continuous learning and improvement. It can open up some new doors with a different perspective or approach.

Stay adaptable

Be willing to revise your plan or goals as circumstances change or new information becomes available. Flexibility and adaptability are essential qualities for success, as they enable you to respond effectively to unforeseen challenges or opportunities. Staying adaptable makes you flow like water and you will find your way through all obstacles. Here are some reasons why staying adaptable is important:

1. Embracing change: Change is an inevitable part of life, and staying adaptable allows us to embrace it rather than resist it. When we are able to adapt to change, we are better equipped to navigate uncertainty and take advantage of new opportunities as they arise.
2. Managing risks: Staying adaptable also helps us to manage risks more effectively. When we are open to new ideas and approaches, we can more easily identify potential risks and develop mitigation strategies.
3. Innovation: Adaptable people are often more innovative, as they are able to identify new ways of doing things and are willing to experiment and try new approaches.
4. Resilience: Adaptable people are more resilient and better able to bounce back from setbacks and failures. They are able to reframe challenges as opportunities for growth and learning and are able to quickly pivot and adapt to changing circumstances.
5. Continuous improvement: Staying adaptable also helps us to continually improve and grow, as we are able to identify areas for improvement and take action to address them.

Staying adaptable is important for achieving success because it allows us to embrace change, manage risks, innovate, build resilience, and pursue continuous improvement. By staying adaptable, we are better able to navigate the challenges and opportunities that come our way, and ultimately achieve our desired outcomes.

Celebrate small victories

Acknowledge and celebrate your achievements, no matter how small. Recognizing your progress can boost your motivation and reinforce your commitment to your goals. Celebrating small victories is important for achieving success for several reasons:

1. Boosts motivation: Celebrating small victories can boost motivation and help to maintain momentum towards larger goals. When we celebrate small successes, we feel a sense of accomplishment, which can help to motivate us to continue working towards our larger goals.

2. Increases confidence: Celebrating small victories can also increase our confidence and self-belief. When we achieve small successes, we start to build evidence that we are capable of achieving our larger goals, which can increase our confidence and belief in our abilities.

3. Reinforces positive habits: Celebrating small victories can help to reinforce positive habits and behaviours that contribute to success. When we acknowledge and celebrate our progress, we are more likely to continue engaging in the behaviours that led to that progress.

4. Creates a positive mindset: Celebrating small victories helps to create a positive mindset and can lead to a more optimistic outlook. By focusing on what we have accomplished rather than what we

have yet to achieve, we cultivate a sense of gratitude and positivity that can help to fuel further progress.

5. Increases resilience: Celebrating small victories can also increase our resilience and ability to cope with setbacks and failures. By focusing on what we have achieved, we are better able to maintain a growth mindset and learn from our experiences, even when things don't go as planned.

Celebrating small victories is important for achieving success because it boosts motivation, increases confidence, reinforces positive habits, creates a positive mindset, and increases resilience. By taking the time to acknowledge and celebrate our progress, we can stay motivated and focused on our goals, and ultimately achieve the success we desire.

These are the few practical strategies you can use to increase your chances of achieving success and maintain the motivation and focus needed to accomplish your goals. Ultimately, the most important strategy for success may vary from person to person, depending on their individual goals, strengths, and challenges. However, by cultivating a growth mindset and adopting other effective strategies, individuals can increase their chances of achieving success in various areas of their lives. Remember, success is a journey that requires persistence, dedication, and ongoing personal growth. With every growth opportunity, you should improve yourself rather than prove yourself.

* * *

8

Conclusion

Final thoughts on the importance of mindset and attitude for success

While talent, education, and intelligence are undoubtedly important factors in achieving success, research has shown that having the right mindset is even more critical. In particular, having a growth mindset can be a powerful predictor of success in various areas of life.

Understanding mindset is crucial for personal growth and development. By cultivating a growth mindset and overcoming limiting beliefs, individuals can overcome obstacles and achieve their goals with persistence and resilience. Building resilience and a positive attitude can help individuals bounce back from setbacks and maintain a sense of motivation and purpose.

Meditation and mindfulness can be powerful tools for developing a growth mindset and building resilience. Through these practices, individuals can learn to manage their thoughts and emotions, reduce stress and anxiety, and cultivate a greater sense of focus and awareness.

To achieve success, individuals must set SMART goals, prioritize their tasks, establish positive habits and routines, monitor their progress, seek feedback and support, and stay adaptable to changing circumstances. Celebrating small victories and learning from setbacks can help individuals maintain momentum and motivation on their journey to success.

By applying the principles of understanding mindset, building resilience, cultivating a positive attitude, overcoming limiting beliefs, and using meditation and mindfulness, individuals can develop the skills and mindset necessary to achieve success in all areas of their lives.

The power of mindset and attitude in achieving success cannot be overstated. Throughout this book, we have explored the concept of mindset and the importance of adopting a growth mindset for success in various areas of life. We have also examined the role of attitude and how developing a positive attitude can contribute to greater happiness, success, and fulfilment.

One of the key takeaways from this book is the importance of challenging limiting beliefs and negative thought patterns. By adopting a growth mindset and reframing negative thoughts into positive ones, we can overcome self-doubt and achieve our full potential. We have also seen that perseverance, resilience, and a willingness to learn from failure are essential for achieving success and overcoming challenges.

We have explored the stories of successful individuals who overcame limiting beliefs and achieved great success, including Oprah Winfrey, J.K. Rowling, and Michael Jordan. These all individuals demonstrated a growth mindset and a positive attitude, and their stories serve as inspiration for anyone looking to overcome obstacles and achieve their goals. These people can serve the great purpose of being your inspiration.

Throughout the book, we have provided practical strategies for developing a growth mindset and positive attitude, including the importance of learning, risk-taking, and perseverance. We have also explored the benefits of meditation, mindfulness, gratitude, and positive self-talk for developing a positive attitude and maintaining a growth mindset.

In addition to personal development, we have examined the role of mindset and attitude in career growth. We have seen that adaptability, resilience, and networking are essential for achieving success in the workplace, and that a growth mindset and positive attitude can contribute to career advancement.

We have also explored the impact of mindset and attitude on mental and physical health. We have seen that a positive mindset and attitude can improve mental well-being, reduce stress, and promote healthy habits. We have also seen that a growth mindset can help individuals to overcome physical challenges and achieve their fitness goals.

In conclusion, our beliefs, thoughts, and attitudes shape our perception of the world around us and determine the actions we take. By adopting a growth mindset and positive attitude, we can overcome self-doubt, challenges, and obstacles to achieve our goals and reach our full potential.

Through the stories of successful individuals who overcame limiting beliefs and achieved great success, we have seen the power of mindset and attitude in action. These individuals demonstrate that a growth mindset and positive attitude are key ingredients for achieving success and happiness in life.

The strategies and insights presented in this book provide a roadmap for developing a growth mindset and positive attitude. From challenging limiting beliefs and negative self-talk to cultivating resilience, perseverance, and self-compassion, these strategies can help us to develop the mindset and attitude necessary for success in various areas of our lives. It is important to remember that developing a growth mindset and positive attitude is an ongoing process. Mindset and attitude are powerful tools that can help us to achieve success, happiness, and fulfilment in life.

* * *

9

Self-Survey

Unlock Your Potential with Our Self-Survey

Are you looking to achieve success in your personal or professional life? The first step is to understand your mindset and attitude towards success. Our self-survey is designed to help you do just that.

By taking our self-survey, you'll gain valuable insights into your mindset and attitudes towards success. You'll discover your strengths and areas for improvement, and gain a deeper understanding of how your mindset can impact your success.

But that's not all. Our self-survey is just the beginning. With its practical insights and guidance, you'll be equipped with the tools and strategies you need to cultivate a growth-oriented mindset and achieve your goals.

So what are you waiting for? Take our self-survey today and unlock your full potential for success!

Do you believe that intelligence and abilities are:
  a) fixed traits that cannot be changed
  b) qualities that can be developed over time

When faced with challenges or setbacks, do you:
  a) give up easily and feel discouraged
  b) persist and find ways to overcome the obstacles

How do you view failure?
  a) as a reflection of your abilities and potential
  b) as a learning opportunity to improve and grow

Do you set clear and specific goals?
  a) rarely or never
  b) often and consistently

How do you manage your time?
  a) get easily distracted and procrastinate
  b) prioritize important tasks and manage time efficiently

How do you respond to feedback and criticism?
  a) get defensive and dismiss it
  b) use it constructively to improve and grow

How do you approach risk-taking?
  a) avoid taking risks and prefer to stay in your comfort zone
  b) take calculated risks in pursuit of your goals

How do you cope with stress and uncertainty?
  a) get overwhelmed and have difficulty coping
  b) have healthy coping mechanisms and strategies in place

How often do you seek out new learning opportunities?
   a) rarely or never
   b) often and consistently

How do you view success?
   a) as a fixed endpoint or destination
   b) as an ongoing process of growth and development

We hope that taking this self-survey has helped you gain a deeper understanding of your mindset and attitude towards success. If you're looking to continue your personal and professional growth journey, we invite you to join us on our website, www.aayatpublications.com.

On our website, you'll find a wealth of resources and content to help you develop a growth-oriented mindset and achieve your goals. From articles and blog posts to e-books and self-assessment tools, we provide a wide range of resources to help you cultivate a positive and proactive attitude towards success.

In addition to our content, we also offer a community of like-minded individuals who are committed to personal and professional growth. Whether you're looking for support, guidance, or inspiration, our community is a great place to connect with others who share your goals and aspirations.

We invite you to join us on www.aayatpublications.com and become part of our community of growth-oriented individuals. Together, we can cultivate the mindset and attitude necessary for success and achieve our full potential.

SELF-SURVEY

** * **

Resources

Inspiration - Carol Dweck: Mindset: The New Psychology of Success

https://jamesclear.com/fixed-mindset-vs-growth-mindset

https://asana.com/resources/limiting-beliefs

https://positivepsychology.com/what-is-resilience/

https://www.mindtools.com/asbakxx/dwecks-fixed-and-growth-mindsets

https://fs.blog/carol-dweck-mindset/

https://www.berkeleywellbeing.com/develop-positive-attitude.html

https://www.successconsciousness.com/blog/positive-attitude/what-is-the-meaning-of-positive-attitude/

Also by Fateh S Chahal

Secret of Everlasting Happiness
A couple's Therapy to Strengthen Your Relationship with Better Communication, Understanding and Space.

A Couple's Therapy To Find Secrets of Everlasting Happiness
The Top 9 Secrets of how to Create Healthy, Happy Relationships